Key Stage Three
History

How to get your free Online Edition

This book includes a **free** Online Edition you can read on your computer or tablet wherever you have an internet connection.

To get it, just go to **cgpbooks.co.uk/extras** and enter this code...

0189 3942 9047 1852

By the way, this code only works for one person. If somebody else has used this book before you, they might have already claimed the Online Edition.

D1354852

Complete Study and Practice

Contents

Contents

Published by CGP

Editors:
Emma Bonney
Heather Gregson
Sabrina Robinson

Contributors:
Steve Buckley, Peter Callaghan, Mark Chambers, René Cochlin, Matt Hardwick,
Kim Hodges, John Pritchard, Warren Turner and Judith Vandervelde.

With thanks to Holly Poynton and Karen Wells for the proofreading.

With thanks to Jan Greenway and Laura Jakubowski for the copyright research.

ISBN: 978 1 84146 391 9

Printed by Elanders Ltd, Newcastle upon Tyne.
Clipart from Corel®

Based on the classic CGP style created by Richard Parsons.

Text, design, layout and original illustrations © Coordination Group Publications Ltd. (CGP) 2014
All rights reserved.

Photocopying more than one chapter of this book is not permitted. Extra copies are available from CGP.
0870 750 1242 • www.cgpbooks.co.uk

How to Use This Book

This book will help you to do the best you can in Key Stage 3 History — it's full of important events, historical sources and practice questions to help you improve your history skills.

History Isn't all Dead and Buried

History isn't all about Kings, Queens and dates — it's full of <u>life changing events</u>.
Just think —

- What would you have done if there was a sudden outburst of bubonic plague?
- Would you have chosen to fight for the Roundheads or the Cavaliers during the Civil War?
- Would you have protested to abolish slavery?

These were all decisions ordinary people had to make, and their outcomes <u>still affect you</u> today.

There are Four Sections in this book

The four sections are:
1) <u>Medieval Britain, 1066-1509</u>
2) <u>Tudors and Stuarts, Britain 1509-1745</u>
3) <u>Industry, Empire and Reform, Britain 1745-1914</u>
4) <u>Britain and the Wider World, 1900 to the Present Day</u>

There are Picture Sources and Written Sources for each topic

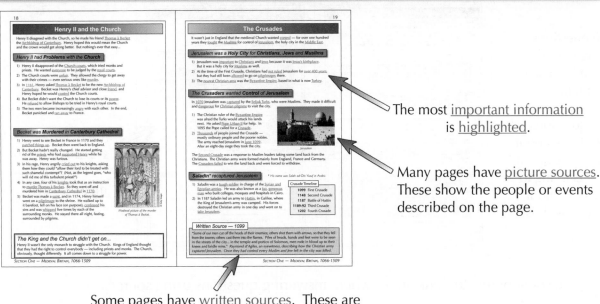

The most <u>important information</u> is <u>highlighted</u>.

Many pages have <u>picture sources</u>. These show the people or events described on the page.

Some pages have <u>written sources</u>. These are usually bits of writing or speeches from the period of history the page is about. They give the point of view of someone who actually lived at the time — or someone who's an expert on the subject.

How to Use This Book

Each section starts with a *Timeline*

At the beginning of each section there is a <u>timeline</u>. This shows all the important events in that section in the order they happened. It shows you how all the different bits of history <u>link together</u>.

All the <u>important events</u> described in the section are shown in the <u>timeline</u>. This is the timeline for Section One, about Medieval Britain.

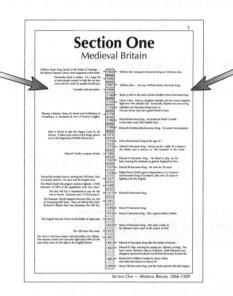

In Sections <u>One</u> and <u>Two</u>, information about <u>Kings</u>, <u>Queens</u> and other <u>rulers</u> is shown on the <u>right</u>. It can be pretty confusing trying to keep track of which monarch was on the throne at a particular time, and of who came before and after them. Look back at this if you get confused.

There are *Lots* of *Questions* that use *Sources*

<u>Sources</u> are a huge part of studying history — that's why we've included loads of questions that include sources to help you practise using them.

A source could be <u>written</u> or it could be a <u>picture</u>.

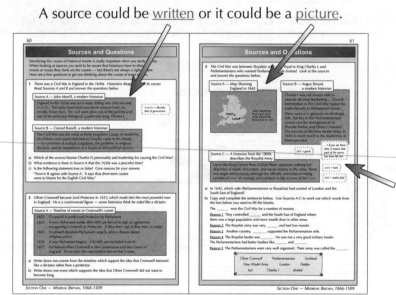

Some questions ask you to <u>find information</u> using the source.

Other questions ask you to think about what <u>impression</u> a source is trying to give us, or about how <u>reliable</u> it is.

There are boxes to <u>explain</u> any words in a source that might be <u>confusing</u>.

Here are some points to think about when answering questions using sources:

- <u>Who</u> wrote or created the source?
- Is the source likely to be <u>biased</u>?
- If there is more than one source, do they <u>agree or disagree</u>, and why might this be?
- <u>When</u> was it written or painted?
- Could the source be <u>inaccurate</u>?

Section One
Medieval Britain

William beats King Harold at the Battle of Hastings — the Bayeux Tapestry shows what happened at the battle. — **1066** — William the Conqueror becomes King on Christmas day.

Domesday Book is written. It's a huge list of what people owned, to help the tax man work out how much tax people should pay. — **1086**

1087 — William dies — his son, William Rufus, becomes King.

Crusaders take Jerusalem. — **1099**

1100 — Rufus is shot in the back and his brother Henry becomes King.

1135 — Henry I dies. Henry's daughter Matilda and her cousin Stephen fight over who should rule. Eventually Stephen becomes King.

1154 — Matilda's son becomes King Henry II. He was clever, but not a good friend to have.

Thomas à Becket, Henry II's friend and Archbishop of Canterbury, is murdered by four of Henry's knights. — **1170**

1189 — Richard becomes King. He leads the Third Crusade to the Holy Land (The Middle East).

1199 — Richard's brother John becomes King. He wasn't very popular.

John is forced to sign the Magna Carta by his barons. It takes away some of the King's power and is the beginning of British democracy. — **1215**

1216 — Henry III becomes King at the age of 7.

1272 — Edward I becomes King. Always up for a fight, he conquers the Welsh and is known as 'The Hammer of the Scots'.

Edward I finally conquers Wales. — **1282**

1307 — Edward II becomes King. He liked to play on his farm, leaving his ministers to govern England for him.

1327 — Edward III becomes King. He rules for 50 years.

1328 — Robert Bruce finally gains independence for Scotland and becomes King of Scotland, after over 20 years of fighting with the English.

Edward III invades France, starting the 100 Years War. It actually lasts for 116 years and the English lose. — **1337**

The Black Death (the plague) reaches England. It kills between 33 and 50% of the population over two years. — **1348**

The first Poll Tax is introduced to pay for the war in France. Everyone over 15 has to pay it. — **1377** — Richard II becomes King.

The Peasants' Revolt happens because they are sick of increasing Poll Taxes. They are led by Wat Tyler. Richard II defeats them but abandons the Poll Tax. — **1381**

1399 — Henry IV becomes King.

1413 — Henry V becomes King. He's a great military leader.

The English beat the French at the Battle of Agincourt. — **1415**

1422 — Henry VI becomes King. He's only a baby so his advisors have most of the power at first.

The 100 Years War ends. — **1453**

The Wars of the Roses begin with the battle at St. Albans. The Houses of York and Lancaster fight each other for the next thirty years for the right to the English throne. — **1455**

1461 — Edward IV becomes King after the Battle of Towton.

1483 — Edward IV dies, leaving his young son, Edward, as King. The boy's uncle, Richard, rules as Protector. Both Edward IV's sons disappear (presumed dead) and Richard becomes Richard III.

1485 — Richard III is killed in battle by Henry Tudor, who takes the throne as Henry VII.

1509 — Henry VIII becomes King, and the Tudor period officially begins.

The Norman Conquest and Beyond

Just after Harold became King of England (King of the Saxons), Vikings invaded at Stamford Bridge. Harold won, but then <u>William</u> of <u>Normandy</u> believed he should be the King and invaded Britain. His troops landed at Pevensey in September 1066.

William **Invaded**, and **Won** the **Battle of Hastings**

Harold <u>marched</u> his <u>tired army</u> back south to meet William, getting a few more soldiers on the way.

1) William moved his army to <u>Hastings</u>.
2) Harold positioned his army to <u>block the road</u> to London.
3) William now had to <u>attack</u> if he wanted to become king.

The <u>Battle of Hastings</u> was fought on <u>14 October 1066</u>. William's army was <u>well trained</u> and had lots of <u>knights</u>. Harold had about the <u>same number</u>, but they were all <u>tired foot soldiers</u>.

1) William tried archers first, then spearmen and then knights.
2) Nothing seemed to be working. Then William got lucky — his <u>Breton allies ran away</u> and some of the <u>Saxons chased them</u>, leaving fewer Saxons to fight against William.
3) The Normans rode them down, and the Saxon line was now thinner.
4) The Norman archers could now <u>shoot at the Saxons</u>.
5) The knights charged the Saxons and Harold was killed — William had won.

The Normans made the <u>Bayeux Tapestry</u> to show their version of events.

© French School/Getty Images

Part of the Bayeux Tapestry

Written Source — 1071

"Seeing his men fleeing, he [William] took off his helmet and cried, 'Look at me well! I am still alive and by God's grace I shall yet prove victor.'" *William of Poitiers, who wrote about the life of William I, describes how William I rallied his troops to make them carry on fighting.*

The Norman Conquest and Beyond

Being King of England Wasn't Easy

William was crowned King on Christmas Day 1066, but his problems were just starting.

1) William built castles to try and take control of the country.

2) It wasn't just being king of the English that was difficult. William had to deal with Viking settlers in the North and the Scots and Welsh, who all had their own leaders, as well as Norman settlers and lords who moved to Britain after the conquest.

3) William ordered the Domesday Book to record everything about England, and to see how much tax he could collect (more about this on p. 6-7).

4) There were three serious rebellions against his rule which he put a stop to — in the North, the South West and in East Anglia.

5) In 1069 some Vikings and northern English men rebelled against William. They failed but William was worried, so he burned and destroyed lots of villages in the North.

Statue of William I at Wells Cathedral in Somerset.

William's Son became the Next King

William the Conqueror died in 1087 after a riding accident. The new King was his son, William Rufus. He was known as Rufus because of his red (ruddy) complexion (Rufus means "red" in Latin).

1) Rufus took control of the English throne.

2) Rufus's reign was bloody, but not a total failure. He taxed people as much as he could and beat off foreign invaders and revolts at home.

3) He conquered Cumbria and Wales and overthrew the Scottish King.

4) Some of his Barons rebelled in support of his older brother Robert, but he beat them off too. Robert then decided to claim Normandy instead and eventually went off to fight in the Crusades (see p. 19).

5) In 1100, Rufus was shot in the back on a hunting trip. Some people think that the chief suspect (Walter Tyrel) was obeying orders from Rufus's younger brother, Henry, who became the next King.

Portrait of William II, from around 1100.

The Normans began to build the Britain we know today...

Some of William I's castles are still standing today, which is pretty impressive as there weren't any cranes, diggers or cement mixers 1000 years ago — the most famous are the Tower of London and Windsor Castle.

The Domesday Book

Twenty years after the Battle of Hastings, William the Conqueror decided to discover <u>who</u> really <u>owned</u> all the <u>land</u> in England. This was basically so he could work out who owed him taxes...

The **Domesday Book** was **Not Popular**

The <u>Domesday Book</u> was basically a <u>big list</u> of who owned what in England. William I used it to calculate <u>how much to tax people</u>. So, clearly some people weren't very happy about this. It was written in <u>1086</u> and asked questions like —

1) How many slaves and freemen are there in your manor?
2) How much is your manor worth?

It even recorded things like <u>how many animals</u> you had on your land. It showed how <u>efficient</u> the Normans were, compared to the Saxons who ruled before them.

The Domesday Book contains so much information that it's actually spread over two books.

Domesday means 'God's Judgement Day' but it wasn't called the Domesday book until the twelfth century.

© Mary Evans Picture Library

The Domesday Book

The **Domesday Book** tells us about **Village Life**

The Domesday Book gives us a pretty good picture of <u>life in the country</u>:

1) The overall population was around <u>one and a half million</u> people, and 90-95% of people lived in rural areas.
2) Villages were small — around <u>300-500</u> people.
3) There were often one or two <u>manors</u> in a village (manors were basically big fortified houses that looked like castles), where a Lord or Baron lived.
4) Peasants living in the villages were mostly "<u>villeins</u>".
5) Villeins had <u>their own small pieces of land</u> to farm, but to pay for them they had to work on the Lord of the Manor's land as well. A system like this where you pay for land <u>with work</u> (not money) is called a <u>feudal system</u>. It makes the landowners very <u>powerful</u>.
6) Villeins had three chances of <u>freedom</u> — they could receive it from the Lord of the Manor, save up enough to buy it, or else run away to a town. If they weren't caught for a year and a day then they became free.

Written Source — 1087

"There was no single hide nor a yard of land nor indeed was one ox or one cow or one pig left out, that was not put down in his record." *This extract is from the Anglo-Saxon Chronicle. It describes the level of detail of the information recorded in the Domesday Book.*

The Domesday Book

The *Domesday Book* also tells us about *Town Life*

Only 100 towns were included in the Domesday Book.

1) The only big places were <u>around cathedrals</u>, such as Lincoln, York and Westminster Abbey. But there were fewer than 10,000 people living in most of these towns.

2) <u>Towns developed</u> around travelling and meeting points such as crossroads or river crossings.

3) Towns attracted villagers and merchants to <u>trade</u>.

4) Craftsmen and merchants formed <u>guilds</u> to protect the quality of their work.

5) Wealthy towns built large <u>defensive walls</u>.

6) Successful towns gained <u>charters</u> setting out the <u>rights of townspeople</u>. These were awarded by the Lord or bought from the King.

A picture showing medieval wall building.

Westminster Abbey

The big towns had huge, impressive cathedrals like Westminster Abbey, but the Normans also built lots of churches in the smaller towns and villages.

The Domesday Book is incredibly <u>important to historians</u>. There's not much <u>written evidence</u> of what life was like for medieval peasants or the lower classes — most writing was about religion or important people. So a book telling us exactly how people lived in every corner of the country is really valuable.

The Domesday Book — Norman record keeping at its best...

The information in the Domesday Book was collected by a small group of commissioners who went around the country and visited the 13,418 places listed in the book. It was then taken back to London and written up neatly by just one monk.

The English Medieval Church

The Catholic Church had a huge impact on everyday life in medieval England. The stuff on this page is dead important to know about, as it affects everything in this period of history.

Christendom was Wherever the Catholic Church was

Medieval England was part of Christendom — all the countries where most people were Christian. Under Christendom, politics and society were closely linked to the Church.

1) Christendom covered the whole of Europe, apart from bits of Scandinavia and some Muslim areas in Spain and southern Italy.

2) This meant that the beliefs and teachings of the Catholic Church controlled the way most people behaved throughout Europe.

3) Nearly everyone would have had some link with the Church:
   • a family member might be a clergyman.
   • they might pay rent to a Church landlord.
   • they might work for the Church.
   • they had to pay annual tithes (taxes) to the Church.

4) People were told they'd go to hell if they didn't support the Church.

People left money to the Church so that prayers could be said to shorten their time in purgatory. (Purgatory was where they'd go before heaven, to have their sins cleansed by fire.)

Another way the Church made money was by selling religious relics. These were things like parts of Jesus' cross, bones of saints and dust from the Holy Land. Because it was really hard to prove these things were real there were lots of people who made money by selling fake relics — including some corrupt clergymen.

Clergy selling religious relics at market

© Mary Evans Picture Library

Written Source — 1095

"Brothers, I speak as a messenger from God. Your fellow Christians in the east desperately need your help. The Saracens have attacked them and pushed deep into Christian land... In the name of God, I beg you all to drive out these foul creatures." *Part of Pope Urban II's sermon in 1095. He was asking men to drive the Saracens out of Jerusalem, which started the Crusades — the Church was so powerful at the time it could start wars (see p. 19-20).*

The English Medieval Church

The **Church** was very **Powerful**

1) For most of the medieval period, the Church was richer than the King was.

2) The clergy didn't have to pay taxes, and ordinary people had to pay them for baptisms, weddings and funerals. People were told that they'd go to hell if they didn't cough up the money.

3) The Church could afford to build impressive stone churches and cathedrals (most other buildings were just made of wood). These stone buildings have often lasted for centuries.

4) Bishops became political figures. Some of them controlled important areas of England (like bits near the Scottish border).

Not everyone thought the Church was great. The Lollards (an English religious group) attacked the Roman Catholic Church's wealth and privileges. They were accused of being heretics (people who hold beliefs that go against what the Church says). Many were burnt at the stake in the early 1400s.

Parish Priests were expected to **Do Loads**

The Church had an organised structure. The Pope in Rome was at the head, and had a network of bishops and senior clergy to help him maintain power. At the bottom was the parish priest.

1) Priests told the villagers what to do and how to behave.
2) Priests were not normally of noble birth.
3) They weren't supposed to get married (though some did).
4) They earned an income from farming done on the church lands (called the glebe).
5) They took services, said mass and heard confession.
6) They were expected to teach local children, and help out the sick and the poor.

Some priests were good — they cared for their parishes and tried to help the poor.

Some priests were bad — there were lots of different ways in which they were bad. Some were greedy, others were lazy. Sometimes priests weren't very well educated so didn't really understand what they were supposed to be doing. Then there were some priests who just cared more about money, women and pleasure than they did about the Church.

The influence of the Church affected everyone...

In the medieval period, religion had a big effect on people's everyday lives. Some men were even willing to risk their lives fighting in religious crusades. It wasn't easy to rebel against the Church — you'd be threatened with hell and purgatory, which don't sound like nice places.

Monks and Monasteries

Lots of people used to go off and become nuns and monks. <u>Dedicating</u> your <u>life to God</u> was seen as the most sacred thing you could do with your life.

Monastic Life has a long History in Britain

Before the Romans came here, most of the population were <u>pagans</u>, and worshipped their own gods.

1) By the <u>early 300s</u> there were already some <u>bishops</u> about in Lincoln, London and York.

2) In 400, St Ninan set up a <u>monastery</u> at Whithorn in Scotland. Monasteries were where monks went to live away from normal society.

3) The <u>Romans</u> left in about 410 and after that Christianity was only really still popular in Wales. The Anglo-Saxons in England were mostly pagan.

4) Then in 597, a missionary called St Augustine landed in Kent. He was the first Archbishop of Canterbury and set up monasteries which followed the 'Benedictine Rule' — i.e. rules St Benedict made for a holy life. Most medieval monasteries after this followed the <u>Benedictine Rule</u>.

5) Another important monastery was set up by St Columba and St Aidan at Lindisfarne in 635.

6) By 1300 there were over 600 monasteries in England.

7) Most monasteries were for men only, so <u>convents</u> were founded for women.

St Benedict had a vision of people living and working together in prayer, isolated from the outside world. He set out rules about how the monks should spend their time, what they could own and what they should wear. Some monks still live according to St Benedict's rules today.

© Mary Evans Picture Library

Portrait of Saint Benedict

Written Source — 529

"We are going to set up a home to serve God and we will never leave it. Eight times a day we will praise God. No one shall own anything — no book, pen, nothing. Monks shall be silent at all times... The normal clothes shall be a cloak and hood".
St Benedict in 529. These were the rules Benedictine monks had to follow.

Monks and Monasteries

There were lots of Different monastic Orders

1) <u>Cluniacs</u> came from the Benedictine abbey at Cluny in France, bringing a <u>really strict form</u> of Benedictine Rule with them.

2) Even stricter were the <u>Cistercians</u>, who were also from France.

3) The <u>Gilbertines</u> were different because they started in England. They had monks and nuns at the same monastery.

4) <u>Carthusians</u> came from France. They were a very strict order who fasted and took vows of silence.

5) Boys as young as <u>7</u> could <u>become monks</u>. Most newcomers joined when they were a bit older though. <u>Vows</u> would be taken at <u>16</u> — they were:
   - <u>Chastity</u> (no wives or girlfriends).
   - <u>Obedience</u> (obey all church orders).
   - <u>Stability</u> (never leave the monastery).
   - <u>Poverty</u> (never own anything).

6) Monks had to go and pray at <u>loads</u> of different times — starting at 2am and ending at 8pm when they went to bed.

Monks were great builders — their buildings were meant to reflect the glory of God. Fountains Abbey in Yorkshire and Furness Abbey in Cumbria are just two of the pretty amazing ruins that have survived and are open to visitors.

Furness Abbey was founded in 1123.

Abbeys earned Extra Money from Pilgrims

1) Many abbeys claimed to own a <u>religious relic</u> such as the bone of a saint or a splinter from Christ's cross. People made <u>pilgrimages</u> to look at them.

2) Pilgrims were also attracted to the <u>tombs</u> of saintly people, such as Thomas à Becket (see p. 18).

3) Pilgrims liked to <u>collect</u> badges and other souvenirs from the shrines they had visited — all of which they had to <u>pay for</u>.

4) The <u>first great work</u> of English literature (i.e. written in English, not Latin) is based around a pilgrimage. It was 'The Canterbury Tales' by Geoffrey Chaucer — an account of a group of pilgrims travelling to the shrine of Thomas à Becket and telling each other stories along the way.

© Time Life Pictures/Getty Images

Illustration of Chaucer from an early edition of the Canterbury Tales.

The vow of celibacy was too much for some monks...

Monks were sometimes responsible for nuns getting pregnant. The Chicksands Priory allowed men and women in the same monastery. I dare you to guess what happened...

Sources and Questions

Sources are an important part of studying history.
Here are some questions to help you to use and apply sources.

1 In 1066, King William I took control of England with an army of just 20,000 Normans.
   That made him the ruler of over a million English people.
   Read the sources below, then answer the questions which follow.

   Source A — A. Briggs, a modern historian

   > He promised to follow existing laws and customs. He acted as
   > owner of all the land. He kept a quarter for himself, gave the
   > Church a quarter and rewarded the Normans with the rest. In 1086,
   > William made every landowner swear an oath of loyalty to him.

   Source B — A modern discussion of Norman forts

   > When the Normans first conquered England they were
   > heavily outnumbered by the Saxons. It was important for
   > them to assert control and demonstrate their power. One
   > way in which they did this was to build forts all over England.
   > They used Saxon peasants as labour to build the forts.

   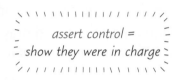
   *assert control =
   show they were in charge*

   a) Read Source A. What did King William do to make himself popular with the following
       groups?
       i) the English people   ii) the Church   iii) the Normans
   b) Why did the Normans build forts in England, according to Source B?

2 There were revolts against the Normans in the early years of William's reign.
   William punished the North of England very harshly for this in 1069. This is known as the
   'Harrying of the North'.

   Source A — Orderic Vitalis, a Norman monk, describes William's 'Harrying of the North'

   > Nowhere else had William shown such cruelty. In his anger he ordered that all crops,
   > herds, possessions and food of every kind should be brought together and burned to
   > ashes. So terrible a famine fell upon the humble and defenceless population, that more
   > than 100,000 Christian folk, both men and women, young and old, died of hunger.

   Source B — The Anglo-Saxon Chronicle describes William

   > Amongst other things, the good order that William established is not to be forgotten. It
   > was such that any man might travel over the kingdom with a bosom full of gold unharmed.

   a) What was the result of William's 'Harrying of the North' according to Source A?
   b) Read Source B. What was one advantage of William enforcing law and order so harshly?

Sources and Questions

3   *The Domesday Book was introduced by King William I in 1086.*
Read Sources A and B carefully, then answer the questions.

Source A — An extract from the Domesday Book, 1086

The Bishop of Coutances holds Olney. There are 24 villagers and 5
smallholders. They have 7 ploughs. There are 5 slaves. There is one
mill valued at 40 shillings. There is enough meadow for 10 ploughs, as
well as woodland and 400 pigs. In total it is valued at twelve pounds.

Source B — A modern historian's view

William's survey of England was useful in many ways. It told him
how rich the country was. This allowed him to work out how much
tax each place had to pay. He could also work out how many
knights each place should send him if he needed to call an army.

a)   How many of the following things did Olney have in 1086?
  i) slaves   ii) ploughs   iii) villagers

b)   Using Source B, describe in your own words two reasons why the Domesday Book was
useful to King William.

c)   Which of the two sources, A or B, is a primary source? Explain your answer.

4   *Some historians have used the Domesday Book to find out about what English society*
was like in medieval England. Read Source A and answer the questions that follow.

Source A — The feudal system in medieval England

The King was the most powerful man in the country and held about a quarter
of the land. The King granted the rest of the country's land to about 200
nobles and 100 important members of the clergy. The nobles and clergy in
turn granted some of their land to knights and gentry. The knights and gentry
allowed peasants to farm their land in return for some of the produce. The least
powerful people in English society were slaves — about 9% of the population.

a)   How many nobles and important clergy did the King grant land to?

b)   Draw a simple diagram of the medieval feudal system. Show the most powerful
person at the top of the diagram and the least powerful people at the bottom.

Sources and Questions

The Church was a major part of medieval life. Here are some sources and questions about the medieval Church to help you practise using historical sources.

5 *Many surviving medieval buildings are churches.*
   Study Source A then answer the questions below.

> **Source A — The accounts for buildings at Westminster Abbey, 1269-1271**
>
> For marble, freestone from Caen and Reigate, ragstone, plaster, chalk the cost is £459 12s 9d. For lead, iron, steel, charcoal, locks, ropes, glass, wax, pitch and for making cement the cost is £140 14s.

a) Where was the freestone used to build Westminster Abbey from?

b) What information in Source A helps explain why medieval churches have lasted longer than other medieval buildings? Consider the following factors: materials, cost, care taken in choosing materials.

6 *Medieval people often went on pilgrimages.*
   Read Sources A, B and C, then answer the questions below.

> **Source A — Tony McAleavy, a modern historian**
>
> People believed that they were more likely to get to heaven if they prayed to the saints. A piece from the body of a dead saint was known as a 'relic'. Relics were thought to have a special power that could help people with their prayers. People would travel many miles to visit a church containing such a relic.

> **Source B — List of relics at Wimbourne Minster in Dorset**
>
> A piece of true cross, a bit of Christ's robe, some hairs from his beard, a piece of the pillar at which he was whipped, a thorn from his crown, a piece of the manger, St William's shoe, St Agatha's thigh bone, one of St Philip's teeth and part of St Mary the Egyptian.

> **Source C — The Life of St Hugh, Bishop of Lincoln, late 1100s**
>
> When Bishop Hugh was at the famous monastery of Fecamp, he got two small pieces of the arm of St Mary Magdalen by biting them from the bone. The monks shouted out, "How terrible. He has stuck his teeth into the bone and gnawed at it, as if he were a dog."

a) Use information from Sources A and B to describe what a relic is.

b) Read Source B. Do you think these relics were genuine? Explain your answer.

c) Do you think that the description of the Bishop of Lincoln's behaviour in Source C is:

   i) true — it is evidence that the Bishop was an unfussy eater.

   ii) made up — maybe the author of this source wanted to show the Bishop in a bad light.

   iii) true — the story is printed in a book, so it is probably true.

Sources and Questions

7 *Some people were unhappy with the state of the medieval Church, for example a group called the Lollards led by John Wycliffe. Read the sources and answer the questions that follow.*

> **Source A — A description of the Archbishop of Canterbury, Thomas à Becket, c.1170**
>
> When Becket crosses the English Channel, he never has less than six ships. Every day he gives away valuable presents of horses, birds, clothes, gold and silver dishes and money.

> **Source B — Taxes for the Church, described by a modern historian**
>
> The peasants paid ten percent of what they earned in a year to the Church. Tithes could be paid in either money or in goods produced by the peasant farmers. A failure to pay tithes, so the peasants were told by the Church, would lead to their souls going to Hell after they had died.

a) Why do you think some people in medieval England would have been angry with the Church, if they heard the information in Source A? Choose from options i)-iii).

i) They might have been angry that they hadn't been given presents by the Archbishop.

ii) They might have been angry that a member of the English clergy would travel across the English Channel to France so often, because it was unpatriotic.

iii) They might have been angry that a member of the clergy should be so rich, when the clergy were supposed to live a religious life of poverty and restraint.

b) Read Source B. Why might peasants have complained about the Church? Give two reasons.

Henry I

Right — Henry I was King after William II. Then he went and left the throne to his daughter Matilda. Not a lot of people liked the idea of a <u>woman ruling England</u>.

Monarchs *were expected to be* Male

1) Monarchs were expected to maintain <u>law and order</u> in the kingdom.

2) Monarchs were expected to be <u>men</u> — lots of people back then thought women shouldn't be in positions of power. There had never been a female monarch.

3) Monarchs had to control the unruly and power hungry <u>groups of barons</u> that they relied upon for support. Most of these barons didn't believe women should rule.

Family tree of the Norman Kings

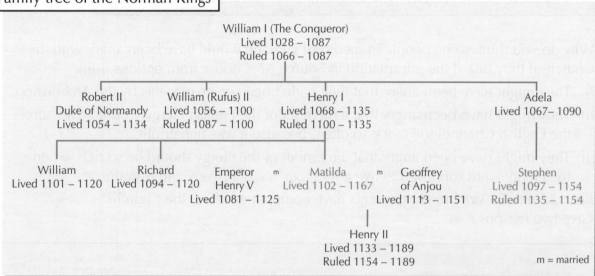

William I (The Conqueror)
Lived 1028 – 1087
Ruled 1066 – 1087

Robert II
Duke of Normandy
Lived 1054 – 1134

William (Rufus) II
Lived 1056 – 1100
Ruled 1087 – 1100

Henry I
Lived 1068 – 1135
Ruled 1100 – 1135

Adela
Lived 1067– 1090

William
Lived 1101 – 1120

Richard
Lived 1094 – 1120

Emperor
Henry V
Lived 1081 – 1125

m

Matilda
Lived 1102 – 1167

m

Geoffrey
of Anjou
Lived 1113 – 1151

Stephen
Lived 1097 – 1154
Ruled 1135 – 1154

Henry II
Lived 1133 – 1189
Ruled 1154 – 1189

m = married

Henry I was a <u>strong</u> monarch who brought <u>stability</u> to England. He helped to lessen the differences between English and Norman society — he even married an English woman.

But in 1120 a boat called <u>The White Ship</u> sank — Henry's only legitimate son William (and two of his other children) were on board. They <u>drowned</u>, along with the rest of the crew, leaving Henry grief-stricken and with no male heir. He decided to make his daughter Matilda heir and made his barons swear an oath of allegiance to her.

Portrait of King Henry I.

Henry I was very educated for his time...

Henry was considered so clever that he was given the nickname 'Beauclerc', which means 'fine scholar'. He was taught Norman-French, Latin and English and he also studied English law. But Henry's real interest was natural history — so much so that he collected animals and had the first zoo in England at his palace in Woodstock.

Matilda and Henry II

Matilda didn't get to be Queen

1) <u>Matilda</u> was <u>betrothed</u> to the German <u>Holy Roman Emperor</u> when she was 8.

2) When he died in 1125, her dad Henry ordered her to marry <u>Geoffrey of Anjou</u>. Geoffrey was the Count of Anjou and Maine, and he later became the Duke of Normandy. Matilda and Geoffrey's marriage was meant to bring peace between England and Normandy.

3) In 1126 Henry got all the English lords, including his nephew Stephen, to <u>acknowledge Matilda</u> as his <u>heir</u>.

4) Henry died in 1135. BUT, Matilda's cousin <u>Stephen</u> got to <u>London</u> before Matilda did, and had himself <u>crowned king</u>.

5) Most nobles wanted <u>Stephen</u> to rule, because he was a <u>man</u>.

6) This basically started off a <u>civil war</u> that lasted for nearly twenty years. <u>Neither side won</u>. Stephen wasn't ruthless enough, and Matilda was a bit too vicious and alienated most of her supporters. She ruled for about 8 months, but it was as '<u>Lady of the English</u>', not Queen.

Portrait of King Stephen.

7) In the end they both got bored and decided that Stephen could <u>remain king</u>, but that <u>Matilda's son</u> Henry should be <u>heir</u> to the throne (Stephen didn't have any sons of his own).

At one point during the war Stephen had Matilda trapped in Oxford Castle, but she managed to escape by putting on a white robe and legging it during a snow storm.

In some books you might find Matilda called Maud. This is because Matilda is the Latin version of the Saxon name Maud.

Henry II Revamped the Court System

Matilda's son became <u>King Henry II</u> in <u>1154</u>. He's remembered in general as having been intelligent and determined (and also pretty moody and mean). He <u>reformed the court system</u>.

1) Until the time of Henry II, medieval courts were really <u>disorganised</u> and <u>complicated</u>.

2) There were loads of <u>different courts</u> competing for power (e.g. Church courts, manor courts).

3) Henry II set up <u>regular royal courts</u> to deal with serious offences such as murder.

4) Judges went around the country to <u>hold trials</u>.

5) <u>Trial by jury</u> became a common way of deciding who was guilty, and things got a lot fairer.

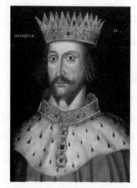

Portrait of King Henry II.

Henry II — a name associated with reform and murder...

Henry II was the first <u>Plantagenet</u> King. (Plantagenet was his dad's nickname because he used to wear a "planta genista" sprig in his hat.) The name "Plantagenet" wasn't actually used by the royal family till about 300 years later though. Lots of historians use the word "Angevins" instead (because Henry's dad was Geoffrey of <u>Anjou</u> — Angevin is the Latin version). So there.

Henry II and the Church

Henry II disagreed with the Church, so he made his friend <u>Thomas à Becket</u> the <u>Archbishop of Canterbury</u>. Henry hoped this would mean the Church and the crown would get along better. But nothing's ever that easy...

Henry II had **Problems** with the **Church**

1) Henry II disapproved of the <u>Church courts</u>, which tried monks and priests. He wanted <u>everyone</u> to be judged by the <u>royal courts</u>.

2) The Church courts were <u>unfair</u>. They allowed the clergy to get away with their crimes — even serious ones like <u>murder</u>.

3) In <u>1161</u>, Henry asked <u>Thomas à Becket</u> to be the new <u>Archbishop of Canterbury</u>. Becket was Henry's chief advisor and close <u>friend</u>, and Henry hoped he would <u>control</u> the Church courts.

4) But Becket didn't want the Church to lose its courts or its <u>power</u>. He <u>refused</u> to allow Bishops to be tried in Henry's royal courts.

5) The two men became increasingly <u>angry</u> with each other. In the end, Becket panicked and <u>ran away</u> to France.

Becket was **Murdered** in **Canterbury Cathedral**

1) Henry went to see Becket in France in 1170 and they <u>patched things up</u>. Becket then went back to England.

2) But Becket hadn't really changed. He started getting rid of the <u>priests</u> who had <u>supported Henry</u> while he was away. Henry was furious.

3) In his rage, Henry angrily <u>cried out</u> to his knights, asking them how they could "allow their lord to be treated with such shameful contempt." (Not, as the legend goes, "who will rid me of this turbulent priest?")

4) In any case, four of his <u>knights</u> took that as an instruction to <u>murder Thomas à Becket</u>. So they went off and murdered him in <u>Canterbury Cathedral</u> in <u>1170</u>.

5) Becket was made a <u>saint</u>, and in 1174, Henry himself went on a <u>pilgrimage</u> to the shrine. He walked up to it barefoot, fell on his face (on purpose), <u>confessed</u> his sins and was <u>whipped</u> five times by each of the surrounding monks. He stayed there all night, fasting, surrounded by pilgrims.

Medieval picture of the murder of Thomas à Becket.

© Hulton Archive/Getty Images

The King and the Church didn't get on...

Henry II wasn't the only monarch to struggle with the Church. Kings of England thought that they had the right to control everybody — including priests and monks. The Church, obviously, thought differently. It all comes down to a struggle for power.

The Crusades

It wasn't just in England that the medieval Church wanted control — for over one hundred years they fought the Muslims for control of Jerusalem, the holy city in the Middle East.

Jerusalem is a **Holy City** for **Christians**, **Jews** and **Muslims**

1) Jerusalem is important to Christians and Jews because it was Jesus's birthplace. But it is a holy city for Muslims as well.

2) At the time of the First Crusade, Christians had not ruled Jerusalem for over 400 years, but they had still been allowed to go on pilgrimages there.

3) The nearest Christian area was the Byzantine Empire, based in what is now Turkey.

The **Crusaders** wanted **Control** of **Jerusalem**

In 1070 Jerusalem was captured by the Seljuk Turks, who were Muslims. They made it difficult and dangerous for Christian pilgrims to visit the city.

Jerusalem

1) The Christian ruler of the Byzantine Empire was afraid the Turks would attack his lands next. He asked Pope Urban II for help. In 1095 the Pope called for a Crusade.

2) Thousands of people joined the Crusade — mostly ordinary people and the poorer nobles. The army reached Jerusalem in June 1099. After an eight-day siege they took the city.

The Second Crusade was a response to Muslim leaders taking some land back from the Christians. The Christian army was formed mainly of the English, French and Germans. The Crusaders failed to win the land back and were forced to withdraw.

Saladin recaptured Jerusalem*

* *His name was Salah al-Din Yusuf in Arabic.*

1) Saladin was a tough soldier in charge of the Syrian and Egyptian armies. He was also known as a fair, generous man who built colleges, mosques and hospitals in Cairo.

2) In 1187 Saladin led an army to Hattin, in Galilee, where the King of Jerusalem's army was camped. His forces destroyed the Christian army in one day and went on to take Jerusalem.

Crusade Timeline	
1099	First Crusade
1148	Second Crusade
1187	Battle of Hattin
1189-92	Third Crusade
1202	Fourth Crusade

Written Source — 1099

"Some of our men cut off the heads of their enemies; others shot them with arrows, so that they fell from the towers; others cast them into the flames. Piles of heads, hands and feet were to be seen in the streets of the city... in the temple and portico of Solomon, men rode in blood up to their knees and bridle reins." *Raymond d'Agiles, an eyewitness, describing how the Christian army captured Jerusalem. Once they had control, every Muslim and Jew left in the city was killed.*

The Crusades and Richard I

The <u>Third</u> and <u>Fourth Crusades</u> didn't manage to win back Jerusalem for the Christians.

Richard I led the *Third Crusade*

Picture from a medieval book showing the coronation of Richard I in 1189.

1) Henry II had <u>four kids</u>. The oldest, <u>Richard</u>, was the next king and after that came his brother <u>John</u>.

2) Richard I was a <u>very brave</u> man. In <u>1189</u> he led the <u>Third Crusade</u> to push Saladin out. The Christian army <u>didn't</u> win back the city of Jerusalem, but they did recapture some <u>ports</u> along the coast, e.g. Acre.

3) Richard was away fighting a lot in the Holy Lands. He spent <u>less than a year</u> in England in the 10 years he was king.

Richard was the King at the time when legend has it that Robin Hood was around. Robin Hood probably wasn't a real person though.

The *Fourth Crusade* never made it to Jerusalem

1) Innocent III became Pope in 1198. One of his main goals was to organise more crusades. In 1202, 11,000 Crusaders met in <u>Venice</u>.

2) The Crusaders attacked a <u>Christian</u> port called Zara and then <u>Constantinople</u> — the Christian capital of the Byzantine Empire.

3) The Crusaders spent <u>3 days</u> looting and destroying Constantinople.

4) The fourth crusade petered out <u>without reaching Jerusalem</u>.

5) Eventually the Latin Kingdom fell apart — <u>Acre</u> was lost in <u>1291</u>.

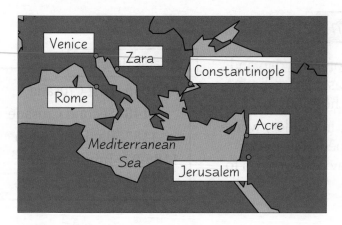

<u>Why they never got to Jerusalem...</u>

When the crusading army arrived in Venice they made a deal to get transport across to Jerusalem.

However, there was an argument about money and the Crusaders couldn't pay all the money the Venetians wanted.

So they agreed to go and capture a few cities for the Venetians instead of paying them — Zara was the first on the list.

King Richard I was called 'The Lionheart'...

This was because of his bravery in battle. Richard has gone down in history as a brave and strong warrior king. He left the country in a bit of a state for his brother John though...

King John

Richard I was killed in <u>1199</u> and had no sons, so his <u>younger brother</u>, John, inherited the throne.

John **Argued** with the **Pope**

1) John fell out with the <u>Pope in Rome</u>, over who should be the next Archbishop of Canterbury.

2) As a result, the Pope <u>excommunicated</u> John (i.e. he expelled him from the church) and declared that he <u>wasn't the rightful king</u> of England.

3) The Pope also banned priests in England from carrying out <u>weddings</u> and <u>christenings</u> for several years whilst he and John <u>argued</u>.

4) This made lots of English people very <u>anxious</u> because they thought they'd go to <u>hell</u>. Lots of them <u>blamed John</u> for this.

King John is given a chalice. The picture was drawn around 1200.

© Hulton Archive/Getty Images

John also fought with the **Barons**

1) Richard <u>spent</u> all of England's <u>money</u> on the crusades. This left John a bit stuck.

2) John needed money in order to <u>pay soldiers</u> to fight wars for him.

3) John had lost his lands in <u>France</u> and <u>wanted them back</u>, but not all the barons were in favour of an expensive war. (When John did fight the French, he was <u>badly beaten</u> twice.)

4) To raise money, John <u>overtaxed</u> the barons, and it wasn't long before they <u>rebelled</u> against him.

Was John **A Bad King?**

Recently, <u>some historians</u> have argued that John <u>wasn't</u> such a <u>bad king</u> after all. Here are some of the arguments on both sides of the debate:

<u>John was a bad king</u>
- He was rude, greedy and had a temper
- He fought with the Pope
- He squeezed as much money as he could out of the barons
- He lost almost all of his land in France

<u>John wasn't a bad king</u>
- He was a fair judge in court
- He was well educated
- Richard's crusades cost lots of money, which wasn't John's fault
- He had enemies because people were trying to steal his crown

John wasn't a very popular king...

John's rule was certainly full of problems, but historians disagree about whether or not this was actually his fault. It's up to you to decide what you think of his time as ruler.

The Magna Carta

In 1214 lots of English barons <u>rebelled</u> against John. This led to the signing of the <u>Magna Carta</u>.

John signed the Magna Carta

The rebelling barons <u>forced John</u> to meet them in a field at <u>Runnymede</u> and sign the <u>Magna Carta</u> in <u>1215</u>. Magna Carta means 'Great Charter', and it centred around three main points —

1) The English <u>Church</u> would be <u>free from state control</u> (i.e. from the King's control) at last.
2) <u>No freeman</u> could be imprisoned or executed without a <u>fair trial</u>.
3) The King <u>couldn't raise taxes</u> without the agreement of barons and bishops first.

© British Library Board

Picture of one of the remaining copies of the Magna Carta.

There were over 63 clauses in total, and the Magna Carta laid the foundation for British democracy.

The Magna Carta paved the way for Parliament

1) The Magna Carta was the first document that <u>officially limited</u> the power of the English <u>monarch</u>.

2) There were a <u>few bits</u> that affected the rights of <u>ordinary people</u>, but it mostly mentions the rights of 'freemen'. Most English people were not classed as 'free' at the time.

3) The Magna Carta was mostly about securing the <u>rights</u> of the <u>barons</u> and the <u>Church</u>.

4) Still, it laid the <u>foundations</u> for <u>future parliaments</u>, because it suggested that the monarch shouldn't have <u>absolute power</u> — the monarch would need <u>permission</u> to do some things.

5) It also said people couldn't be imprisoned without a <u>trial</u>, which was the start of our modern <u>legal system</u>.

Written Source — 1215

"No free man shall be taken or imprisoned or dispossessed, or outlawed or exiled, or in any way destroyed, nor will we go upon him, nor will we send against him except by the lawful judgement of his peers or by the law of the land." *Clause 39 of the Magna Carta setting out the legal rights of free men — this was the start of our modern legal system.*

Relations with the Rest of Britain

During the Middle Ages, the British Isles was <u>not one nation</u>, and <u>not</u> always <u>peaceful</u>. Several English monarchs — particularly <u>Edward I</u> — fought to try and get it all under their <u>control</u>.

The English Kings **Tried** to conquer **All of Britain**

Wales

1) The Normans took over <u>bits of Wales</u> when they first conquered England. But, because of the mountains, Wales was <u>hard to control</u>.

2) <u>Edward I conquered Wales</u> in the 1270s and 80s and built <u>castles</u> there to help control it.

3) Though there were still many revolts against the English, Wales was <u>under English control</u> by Henry VII's day in around 1500.

Ireland

1) The English first got involved in Ireland when <u>Dermot McMorrough</u> (King of Leinster) lost his throne, and asked <u>Henry II</u> to <u>help</u> him get it back.

2) Henry built <u>castles</u> and sent <u>knights</u> to help Dermot. Most Irish chieftains seemed <u>quite happy</u> with this. Dermot offered Henry an <u>oath of loyalty</u> in return for his help.

3) <u>Irish chieftains</u> gave <u>allegiance</u> to the King of England from <u>1172 onwards</u>

Scotland

There was a lot of argument about <u>whether Scotland</u> was a <u>free country</u>. The English thought the Scots owed the King of England an oath of loyalty, but not all the Scots agreed.

1) <u>Edward I</u>, the "Hammer of the Scots", conquered Scotland at the end of the 1200s.

2) But the fighting (and campaigns in Wales) left Edward <u>short of money</u>, so he could not afford to build <u>castles</u> to hold the land.

3) Within a year, <u>rebellions</u> had started across Scotland, and they managed to <u>defeat Edward's forces</u> in battle when he first tried to put them down.

4) <u>Robert the Bruce</u> freed Scotland by 1328, and ruled as its king.

5) Throughout the Middle Ages there were <u>lots of border raids</u> between the English and Scots, involving <u>fighting</u> and <u>theft</u>.

Written Source — 1297

"Now are the islanders all joined together, and Scotland reunited to the royalties of which King Edward is proclaimed lord. Cornwall and Wales are in his power, and Ireland the great at his will." *The Chronicle of Peter Langtoft, 1297. It's talking about how Edward I conquered different parts of England, bringing them under his rule.*

Sources and Questions

It's important to remember that sources can be biased — this affects the message they give. You need to think about how a source could be biased when using it.

1   In medieval England the Archbishop of Canterbury was important and powerful.
    In 1170 the King, Henry II, quarrelled with the Archbishop of Canterbury, Thomas à Becket.
    Read Sources A and B, then answer the questions.

Source A — R. J. Unstead, a modern historian

Henry II was a strong King. He made the barons obey him and pulled down some of their castles. He also tried to force the clergy, who were powerful, to obey his rules. Thomas à Becket would not do so, and for a long time he argued with the King. Henry, in a fit of temper, caused some of his knights to kill Becket in Canterbury Cathedral. Later, he was sorry for this deed.

Source B — An eyewitness account of the death of Becket

In fury, the Knights called out, "Where is Thomas à Becket, traitor to the King?". He came down and in a clear voice said, "I am here, no traitor to the King, but a priest".

a)   What evidence does Source A give that Henry II was a strong king?

b)   What reason does Source A give for the quarrel between the King and the Archbishop, Thomas à Becket?

c)   Do you think the author of Source B is sympathetic to the knights or to Thomas à Becket? Give reasons for your answer.

2   Jerusalem is a holy city for both Christians and Muslims. In the Middle Ages European rulers fought Crusades to try and capture Jerusalem. The third of these Crusades was led by the English King, Richard the Lionheart. Read Sources A and B, then answer the questions below.

Source A — A description of the Third Crusade by a modern historian

The English King [Richard the Lionheart] was often ill, and there were times when Christian soldiers had to eat grass, so badly did they suffer starvation. And the Lionheart never entered Jerusalem. Exhausted by battle, and having made a treaty with Saladin, he knew he could not fight any more.

Saladin = an Islamic war leader who fought against the Crusaders

Source B — Ian Dawson, a modern historian

Richard and the Crusaders did not capture Jerusalem but that does not mean the Crusade was a failure. Certainly Saladin and the Muslims still held the Holy City but the Crusaders had achieved some successes.

a)   What information in Source A suggests that the Third Crusade was a failure?

b)   Does Source B agree with Source A that the Third Crusade was a failure? Give reasons for your answer.

c)   The statement that Richard the Lionheart "knew he could not fight any more" in Source A is —

   i)   a fact — the historian knows what Richard was thinking.

   ii) a guess — the historian can only imagine what Richard was thinking.

Sources and Questions

3 *Salah al-Din (Saladin) is one of the heroes of Arab history, but interpretations of famous people are often different. Read Sources A and B, then answer the questions below.*

Source A — A description of Saladin by Z. Oldenbourg

> This extraordinary man's behaviour was anything but saintly. He was not incapable of cheating. He was calculating, cold and unscrupulous. He managed to put a good face on even his most questionable actions.

Source B — Fiona Macdonald, a modern historian, describes Richard the Lionheart and Saladin

> Why are Richard and Saladin still so famous? Both were strong and resourceful characters. Both risked personal danger with courage and good humour. Both inspired immense loyalty and devotion among the men who fought with them. Both achieved great success in war. Above all, they both possessed qualities — such as courtesy, generosity and bravery — which men who fought on both sides during the crusades valued and admired.

a) List Saladin's bad qualities from the information in Source A.

b) List Saladin's good qualities from the information in Source B.

4 *In 1215, 500 knights attacked the Tower of London because they were angry about high taxes. They forced King John to sign the Magna Carta.*

Source A — A summary of the main points of the Magna Carta

> 1) No freemen will go to gaol without a fair trial and all trials should be held quickly.
> 2) Taxes which are not fair will stop and the King will not ask for extra taxes.
> 3) The Church will be free from interference by the King.
> 4) Merchants will not be subjected to unfair taxes.

Source B — Dr. Mike Ibeji, a modern historian

> The popular image of King John is of a classically bad King. A scheming, untrustworthy coward, consumed by greed. His acts of cruelty are well documented. He hanged and starved 28 hostages and starved to death William de Braose's wife and son in a royal prison.

a) Source A contains the main points of the Magna Carta. Rewrite them in your own words.

b) How does Source B show that King John was cruel?

SECTION ONE — MEDIEVAL BRITAIN, 1066-1509

Sources and Questions

5 *Wales was conquered by the English King Edward I in the 1280s.*
Read the sources and answer the questions that follow.

Source A — Chepstow Castle in Wales

Chepstow Castle was built in 1067 and was in use until the 17th century. It was part of a chain of castles built along the English-Welsh border.

Source B — A historian describes the March Lords

The March Lords held most of the border territories between England and Wales during the medieval period. They were very powerful English Lords, with the power to build castles and wage wars. This system was important to the English, as it meant that frequent rebellions in Wales could be quickly dealt with.

a) Looking at Sources A and B, which of the following statements do you think is most accurate?

   i)   The English used diplomacy and other peaceful methods to take control of Wales.

   ii) The English controlled Wales by force — by building castles and making local lords powerful.

   iii) The English King tried to keep the March Lords under control by limiting their power.

b) Why do you think the March Lords were important to England and were given so much power?

Sources and Questions

6 *In 1296, Scotland rebelled against the English King Edward I.*
Read Sources A, B and C, and answer the questions below.

Source A — The Scottish rebellions

The first Scottish war of independence struggled partly due to divisions in Scotland. The two leaders, Robert the Bruce and John Comyn, were enemies. In 1306 Bruce angrily killed Comyn, after he had betrayed Bruce to Edward I of England. Because the Scottish lords and clans constantly switched sides and fought with each other, they were bound to have trouble uniting and staying together for any long period of time. This made winning a long war against England more difficult.

Source B — The Scottish clan system

The Scottish population was divided into literally hundreds of clans. These clans acted as close family communities in times of peace. They protected and cared for their members. In times of war, they fought together as a regiment of soldiers in the army. Whilst this system was very useful for raising large armies quickly, it also meant that there wasn't much loyalty between the clans, who often fought each other. By bribing and separating certain clans, the English were able to weaken many Scottish rebellions.

Source C — An account of the attack on Berwick

In 1296, the people of Berwick-upon-Tweed refused to surrender to Edward I. His troops attacked the city. In revenge for their refusal to surrender, Edward massacred the population and sacked the town.

massacre = savage killing of a large group of people

sacked = burned and looted

a) Read Sources A and B. What were the advantages and disadvantages of the clan system?

b) Look at the sources. What could English kings do to try and put down rebellion in Scotland? Explain your answer.

c) Read Sources A, B and C. Give two reasons why a Scottish chief might have chosen to fight for the English king, Edward I.

d) What do the sources suggest that life was like for Scottish people during the medieval period? Choose your answer from options i)-iii) below.

   i) Life was hard for Scottish people. They were constantly under attack and had no-one to protect them.

   ii) Life for medieval Scots was hard. There was a lot of war and violence, but people were protected by their clan, who made sure that everyone had food and help when they needed it.

   iii) Life was pretty easy for Scottish people. There wasn't really much violence, and it didn't affect the common people.

The Black Death

We can't be sure exactly how many people died of the Black Death, but historians think it might have been as many as <u>half</u> of the whole British population. That's a lot of people.

Between **33 and 50%** of the population **Died**

1) Plague probably killed between a third and half of the <u>total population</u> of the British Isles.

2) Bubonic plague was <u>spread by fleas</u> which were carried by black rats.

3) Pneumonic plague affected the lungs and <u>breathing</u>. Some historians suggest other diseases were also involved — for example, anthrax.

4) Many people were already weakened due to famine — poor summer weather led to <u>poor harvests</u>.

Plague Timeline

Summer 1348	Bubonic plague travels across the south of England.
September 1348	Plague hits London.
January 1349	Parliament decides to stop meeting.
Spring 1349	Plague now spread into East Anglia, Wales and the Midlands.
Summer 1349	Plague hits the North and Ireland.
1349	The Scots raid Durham while England is weak.
1350	The plague hits Scotland but eases off in London.
1361-64, **1368**, **1371**, **1373-75**, **1390**, **1405**	Plague comes back.

© Mary Evans Picture Library

This medieval picture shows people praying for someone dying of the plague.

People at the time didn't realise how the plague was caused or spread. Some people thought it could be caught from the smell from diseased people, which is why the people in this picture are covering their noses.

The Black Death — not a nice way to die...

The symptoms were nasty — sweating, fever, vomiting, red and black spots, coughing, sneezing and breathing problems. Painful lumps called buboes would appear in your armpits and groin. If you were lucky you died in 1 or 2 days. Some people spent 5 or 6 days in total agony.

The Black Death

People had **Different Explanations** for the Black Death

People in medieval times had no idea about germs — they had their own explanations.

1) Some people thought it was an <u>act of God</u>, and that they were being punished for their sins. People thought their very way of life was being punished.

2) Some people were very <u>superstitious</u>, and thought it was the result of a curse or an evil spirit.

3) Some people thought they were being <u>poisoned</u>. Different groups and individuals were blamed, e.g. the Jews and the poor.

> Medieval people tried all sorts of different tricks to stop themselves getting the plague. Some people carried herbs around with them, others carried flowers. Some people burnt sweet smelling wood in their houses, and some people just prayed to God.

It had **Social** and **Economic Benefits** for **Survivors**

1) Initially some people <u>blamed the poor</u> for the Black Death. It took a while for the King and the nobility to realise that it would affect them too.

2) Killing off so much of the population did actually <u>make life better</u> for the majority of people in the end because it made the survivors <u>more valuable</u>.

3) Before the plague struck, poor people had been <u>forced</u> to work on their local Lord's land, but now they could ask for <u>extra wages</u> and <u>better treatment</u> because the Lords really needed the peasants they had left.

4) Survivors were also able to <u>buy</u> or <u>rent</u> the <u>spare land</u> when other villagers died.

5) It speeded up the breakdown and end of the feudal system, and meant that the <u>ordinary peasants</u> had more <u>freedom</u>.

> It wasn't long before Parliament tried to force the workers to accept lower wages. However, most landowners ignored the new laws and carried on paying workers the higher wages.

Written Source — 1349

"Because many people have died in this plague, some workers will not serve unless they get excessive wages." *From Close Roll 23 (a Close Roll is a record of a royal letter) of Edward III. Workers now knew they could demand higher wages because so many people died from the plague there were fewer people to work the land.*

The Peasants' Revolt

So many people died from the Black Death that society changed. The peasants who survived had more money and more land, which caused the ruling classes some problems.

No one wanted to be Bossed Around any more

1) The feudal system was collapsing. Feudal dues were being replaced by money-rent systems. (See p. 6 for a reminder about the feudal system.)

2) The Black Death had led to a shortage of workers (because so many of them died) and peasant labour was in high demand.

3) The peasants thought this situation was great — they had some privileges now.

The Church was also becoming Unpopular

1) Some peasants were forced to work for the Church. These peasants had to do a lot of their work without getting paid, as it was thought that they were doing 'God's work'.

2) Also, everyone had to pay tithes (religious taxes) to the Church — one tenth of everything they produced or earned.

3) Most people (even landowners) were unhappy that bishops were so wealthy, while normal people had to pay loads of taxes.

The Raising of Taxes made everyone Angry

John of Gaunt was King Richard II's uncle. Richard was only 10 when he became King, so John ruled for him. He kept introducing more taxes to pay for the army. Everyone started to get angry —

1) 1377 — John introduced a Poll Tax (a tax where everyone had to pay the same amount) in order to finance a war with France. Everyone over 15 years old had to pay 4 pence (not much now, but it would have been a pretty big deal then).

2) 1379 — John introduced a second Poll Tax that asked for more money.

3) 1381 — A third Poll Tax was introduced. This was the straw that broke the camel's back.

4) People hid in forests or fought taxmen who arrived to collect 12 pence off everyone.

5) The rebellion started off in Kent and Essex in June 1381, and was led by Wat Tyler.

> The Peasants' Revolt started in Brentwood, Essex, when some of the villagers refused to pay a tax collector. The unrest soon spread to other villages in Kent, Suffolk, Hertfordshire and Norfolk. Armed villagers attacked manors and religious houses. It was then that some of them decided to march on London.

Written Source — 1381

"We are men formed in Christ's likeness, but we are kept like animals. No lord should have lordship: it should be divided among all men, except for the King's own lordship." *Part of Wat Tyler's speech at Blackheath on 13 June 1381. Basically, what he was saying was that his supporters thought all men, except Kings, should be equal and not owned by other men.*

The Peasants' Revolt

The King Stopped the Revolt

1) <u>King Richard II</u> was still only 14 when the revolt was going on.

2) The rebels <u>killed</u> the <u>Archbishop of Canterbury</u> and burned the Savoy Palace.

3) Richard met the rebels and <u>promised</u> that all of their demands would be met.

4) But, as soon as most of the peasants had gone home, lots of the <u>rebel leaders</u> were <u>hanged</u> and <u>Wat Tyler</u> was <u>beheaded</u>.

5) The Poll Tax was <u>abandoned</u>, but peasants were forced back under the <u>control of the lords</u>.

The Main Events of the Rebellion

June 1381	Rebels from Kent and Essex march on London and are joined by some of London's poor.
14th June	Richard II meets rebels and agrees to some demands. Some rebels go home. Other rebels burn down the Savoy Palace, and murder the Archbishop and stick his head on a spike.
15th June	Richard meets rebels again and agrees to most demands. A fight breaks out and Wat Tyler is stabbed. He is taken to hospital and later arrested.
July 1381	Revolt is over. Wat Tyler is beheaded and other rebel leaders are hanged. Richard ignores his promises to the rebels.

© Mary Evans Picture Library

Richard II meeting the rebels.

Wat Tyler was stabbed by one of the King's men at their second meeting with Richard II. Wat was taken to hospital by some of his supporters, but the Mayor of London found Wat, took him to Smithfield, beheaded him and put his head on a spike.

The Peasants' Revolt shows how the feudal system was failing...

This was a pretty important event. It shows how the feudal system was falling apart after 300 years. It also shows some people did get angry at the Church, and weren't afraid to show it.

The Hundred Years War

Before 1066, it was the Vikings who tried to conquer France. After 1066, it was the English.

The **Hundred Years War** had **Short** and **Long Term Causes**

Long Term Causes

1) William I conquered England in 1066. He already controlled Normandy, in France.
2) Henry II (ruled 1154-1189), William's great grandson, controlled Normandy, Anjou (which he inherited from his father), and Aquitaine (which he got by marriage).
3) King John (see p. 21) then lost Normandy and Anjou in 1204, leaving only Aquitaine. After this, English monarchs wanted to get back the old English lands in France.

Short Term Causes

1) Edward III became King of England in 1327.
2) In 1328, the King of France died, leaving no son and heir. He was Edward III's uncle on his mother's side, so Edward felt he should be King of France. Instead, it went to one of his uncle's cousins, Philip VI.
3) France had also promised to help the Scots in their fight against English intervention, including Edward III.
4) Philip then claimed Aquitaine. Edward was furious.
5) By 1337, Edward was ready to fight the French.
6) The fighting lasted until 1453, and became known as the Hundred Years War.

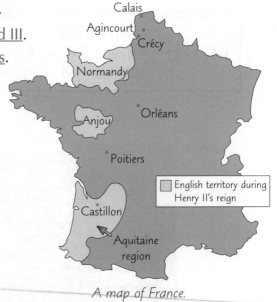

A map of France.

Major Events of the Hundred Years War	
1346	Battle of Crécy (English victory)
1346-7	Siege of Calais (English victory)
1356	Battle of Poitiers (English victory)
1415	Battle of Agincourt (English victory)
1428-9	Siege of Orléans (French victory)
1453	Battle of Castillon (French victory)

The **English** had **Success** to start with

1) The longbow was the most effective weapon by this the 1340s. Edward's officials went round the country recruiting skilled archers.
2) The English archers won comfortably at Crécy in 1346. The longbows were far more effective than the French crossbows.
3) The English army then headed north to Calais and, after a year, they took the city. This became a useful English operations base for the rest of the war.
4) After a break of several years (during which time the Black Death hit both countries), the fighting continued at Poitiers with another English victory.

The Hundred Years War

England had two Great Military Leaders

Edward the Black Prince

1) Edward III's eldest son was known as Edward the Black Prince, possibly because of his dark armour.

2) He was an exceptional military leader, and led the armies at Crécy and Calais in 1346.

3) Edward won a decisive victory at the Battle of Poitiers. He also captured the King of France and sent him back to England. He then charged the French such a high ransom that they couldn't afford to buy him back. Without a King, the French were significantly weakened.

Henry V

1) Henry V was king from 1413 to 1422.

2) He was a great soldier and military leader.

3) At Agincourt in 1415 the French army was five times bigger than his army, but he still managed to beat them in under three hours.

4) Henry now controlled most of northern France.

Portrait of Henry V.

The Tables Turned at Orléans

© DEA / G. DAGLI ORTI / Getty Images

Joan of Arc, from an illustration in a 1505 manuscript.

1) In 1428, English troops attacked Orléans. This was France's strongest military position at the time.

2) The siege lasted for over six months. The English had the upper hand for most of this time.

3) Then, in April 1429, a French peasant girl named Joan arrived. She claimed to have had visions in which she was told to save the French from the English.

4) The French allowed Joan of Arc to lead a group of men, and she rallied the troops so successfully that they drove the English back. The French now had the advantage in France and slowly pushed the English forces out altogether.

5) Henry VI (who ruled from 1422-1461) sent a force to Castillon in 1453 to try and reclaim some territory, but it was unsuccessful.

6) After that, the only English territory in France was Calais.

The fighting wasn't going on for the whole time...

The Hundred Years War wasn't one long, constant battle. There were long breaks in the fighting where tensions would settle down for months or even years at a time, before building up again to another fight. In the end, the English didn't manage to take back lands in France.

The Wars of the Roses

The <u>Wars of the Roses</u> is the name given to the period from 1455-1485 when the
<u>House of Lancaster</u> and the <u>House of York</u> fought one another for the English throne.

There were **Several Causes** of the conflict

*A 'house' is a noble family
and all its descendants.*

1) <u>Claims to the throne</u> — both houses had a legitimate claim to the English throne
because they were both descended from Edward III (see the family tree below).

2) <u>Powerful nobles in England</u> — lots of lords and nobles had their own private armies.
Arguments between them often led to battles.

3) <u>Henry VI's failings in France</u> — Henry lost most of England's lands in France (see p. 33),
which upset lots of the English nobles and they started blaming one another.

4) <u>Henry VI's health</u> — Henry also suffered from mental illness. From 1454-5 Richard, Duke
of York, ruled for him as Protector. When Henry recovered, Richard didn't want to give up
his power, and the Wars of the Roses began.

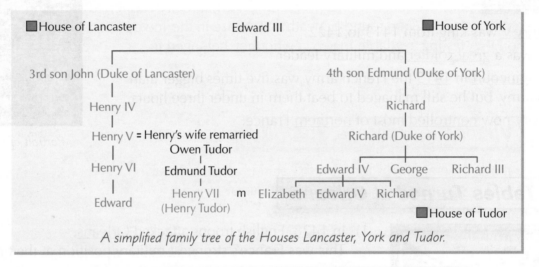

A simplified family tree of the Houses Lancaster, York and Tudor.

*The Wars of the Roses got their name from the emblems of the
two houses — the Red Rose of Lancaster and the White Rose of York.*

The **Wars** lasted for about **30 Years**

The <u>battles</u> caused a lot of <u>disruption</u> when and where they happened, but once
the troops left, people carried on their lives pretty much as <u>normal</u>. The Wars
were mostly about which <u>powerful families</u> would control <u>government</u>.

Timeline of the Wars of the Roses

1455	First battle at St. Albans. Victories go both ways for the next few years.
1461	Edward, the Duke of York's son, wins the throne and rules as Edward IV.
1471	Battle of Tewkesbury. Edward IV destroys the Lancastrian force and Henry VI's son, Edward, is killed. Henry VI dies himself weeks later.
1483	Edward IV dies, leaving the throne to his young son, Edward V. His uncle, Richard III, rules as Lord Protector. Edward V and his younger brother go missing.
1485	Richard III dies in battle fighting Henry Tudor, who takes the throne as Henry VII.

The Wars of the Roses

We Don't Know what happened to Edward IV's Sons

1) Edward IV had ten children — seven daughters and three sons.
   Two of his sons survived him — Edward, his heir, and Richard.

2) Before Edward IV died in 1483, he named his brother, Richard III,
   as Lord Protector, because young Edward was only twelve.

3) Richard had both his nephews sent to the Tower of London, supposedly to keep them safe.

4) By the summer, the princes were seen less and less. Eventually they disappeared from
   public view altogether. It's assumed that they died.

5) Rumours started that Richard had the boys murdered. He certainly had a motive, as their
   death secured his own right to the throne. Richard became King Richard III.

6) Two years later, Richard was killed in battle by Henry Tudor, who then ruled as Henry VII.

7) No evidence has ever been found which proves what really happened to them. In 1674,
   two small skeletons were found beneath a staircase in the Tower, but, unlike today, there
   was no DNA testing available to prove who they belonged to.

Henry VII tried to Restore Stability

Henry VII made several moves to stabilise England after the Wars of
the Roses and protect the throne for his descendants.

Portrait of Henry VII.

1) He married Edward IV's daughter Elizabeth, uniting his
   family with the House of York. This is why the Tudor Rose is a
   combination of the white and red roses of York and Lancaster.

2) Henry married his daughter to James IV of Scotland, and his
   eldest son to Catherine of Aragon, daughter of the Spanish King.
   The marriages strengthened relationships with these countries.

3) He chose good advisors based on their own talents.

4) He was very good with money. England was almost
   bankrupt in 1485, but he restored its fortune, getting
   as much money as he could from royal land and
   introducing a tighter taxation system for the nobles.

5) He recruited Justices of the Peace, to enforce
   law and order throughout England.

6) Henry VII died in 1509. His son, Henry VIII, inherited the throne.

Henry VII restored some peace after the wars...

In 1455, England had just come out of the Hundred Years War — and headed straight into
another war on home soil. It's maybe not surprising that Henry VII was so desperate for a bit
of calm afterwards — and he did a pretty good job of protecting the throne for his family.

36

Sources and Questions

1 *In 1348 a deadly disease arrived in Britain. It was called 'The Black Death' or 'the plague' and nine out of every ten people who caught it died.*

Source A — A survivor of the plague describes the disease, c. 1350

By God's will, this evil led to a strange and unwonted kind of death. The flesh was puffed and swollen.

c. = circa, which means "about." It's used when the exact date isn't known. unwonted = strange

Source B — A description of the causes of the plague from the 1300s

In this year 1348, in Melcombe, in the county of Dorset two ships came alongside. One of the sailors from Gascony has brought with him the seeds of a terrible pestilence.

Gascony = French province pestilence = epidemic of a deadly disease

Source C — The Italian writer Boccaccio described the symptoms of the plague in 1348

Both men and women were affected by a sort of swelling in the groin or under the armpits which reached the size of a common apple or egg. These boils began in a little while to spread all over the body. Later, the appearance of the disease changed to black or red patches on the arms or thighs. These blotches quickly led to death.

a) Complete the following sentence by choosing one of the options i)-iii).

The statement in Source A that the Black Death is God's will is...

i) fact   ii) a likely explanation   iii) opinion

b) Compare Source A and Source B. Which explanation is based on religion, and which on observation?

c) How did the symptoms of the Black Death change over time, according to Source C? Make your answer as detailed as you can.

---

2 *In 1381, many peasants in England revolted. Read Source A and answer the questions below.*

poll tax = a tax where everyone pays the same amount.

Source A — Events of the 1381 Peasants' Revolt

- In 1381 Parliament tried to levy a poll tax of a shilling per person. It was the third poll tax since 1377. People who couldn't afford it were imprisoned.

- There were risings against the tax in Essex, Norfolk and Kent fuelled by discontent about the tax, the feudal system and the war with France. Wat Tyler and John Ball led the uprisings.

- The rebels marched into London. They made a demand that peasants should be freed from the feudal system. The King made some promises to make most of the rebels return home.

- Some rebels remained in London and ran rampage, killing rich men and clergy. They were defeated, and the rebel leaders, Wat Tyler and John Ball, were killed.

a) Name three things that were making people unhappy and led them to take part in the Peasants' Revolt.

b) Using information from Source A, write a short paragraph describing the events of the Peasants' Revolt in your own words.

Section One — Medieval Britain, 1066-1509

Sources and Questions

3 *Joan of Arc was a peasant girl who rallied the French troops at the Siege of Orléans, an important victory for the French in the Hundred Years War.*

Source A — A Letter from Joan of Arc to the English, 1429

King of England, if you do not [leave France], I am a chieftain of war, and in whatever place I meet your people in France, I shall make them leave...And if they will not obey, I will have them all put to death. I am sent here by God, the King of Heaven, body for body, to drive you out of all France.

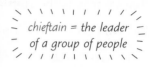
chieftain = the leader of a group of people

Source B — A medieval account of Joan of Arc, c. 1500

At this time a young girl born in Lorraine, the daughter of a poor farmer, came to the Dauphin...In her native village she guarded sheep...She spoke so well that the Dauphin kept her at his court and set her up in great state. This astonished most people because they considered Joan just a simple and foolish girl.

Lorraine = a region in France

Dauphin = the heir to the French throne

a) Using Source A, why did Joan of Arc believe it was her duty to fight the English?

b) What does Source B suggest about how people felt when Joan of Arc first arrived at court?
    i) they loved her   ii) they were afraid of her   iii) they didn't believe her.

c) Looking at Sources A and B, which of the following statements do you think is most accurate?
    i)   Source A suggests that Joan of Arc was not a very strong leader, whereas Source B suggests she could be a great threat to the English armies in France.
    ii) Source A suggests that Joan of Arc was determined to drive the English out of France at any cost, whereas Source B suggests that she seemed an unlikely heroine at first.

4 *For thirty years the Houses of York and Lancaster fought one another for the English throne. This period is known as the Wars of the Roses.*

Source A — The Battle of Tewkesbury, from a 15th century manuscript

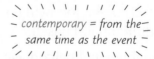
contemporary = from the same time as the event

Source B — A contemporary account of the Battle of Tewkesbury

In the victory of battle, many immediate blows were dealt and men were slain; Edward, the Prince, was captured as he was fleeing to the town guardians, and killed in the field.

Is the statement below supported by Sources A and B? Give reasons for your answer.
"The Battle of Tewkesbury was a violent episode in the history of the Wars of the Roses."

Summary Questions

Wow — our history is pretty gory really. Lots of gruesome murders and things. You'll need these facts and figures at your fingertips if you're going to get anywhere with history, so keep going through these questions until you've got it all sussed.

1) What year was the Battle of Hastings?

2) Who was crowned King of England after the Battle of Hastings?

3) Name two places that William Rufus conquered.

4) What was the Domesday Book and when was it written?

5) In your own words, explain what a "villein" was.

6) What were towns like at the time of the Domesday Book? (Try to sum them up in a sentence.)

7) What is purgatory?

8) Who was richer for most of the medieval period — the King of England, or the Church?

9) Write a paragraph describing the role of a parish priest.

10) What were the four vows that were taken by monks?

11) Who did Henry I decide should be his heir after The White Ship sank in 1120?

12) Explain in three sentences what actually happened after Henry I died.

13) What did Henry II do to make the court system better?

14) Who was Thomas à Becket, and why was he killed?

15) What is the name of the holy city the Crusaders wanted to take over?

16) Who led the Third Crusade?

17) Which religious figure did King John argue with? What happened as a result?

18) Where and when was King John forced to sign the Magna Carta?

19) What were the three main issues dealt with by the Magna Carta?

20) Which king of England conquered Wales in the 1270s and 1280s?

21) Which of the following best sums up medieval relations between England and Scotland?
   a) difficult and unsettled   b) peaceful   c) they had no relations

22) Roughly what percentage of people in Britain died because of the Black Death?

23) Write a paragraph to explain how the Black Death actually made things better for the survivors.

24) What were "tithes", and who had to pay them?

25) In what year was the Peasants' Revolt led by Wat Tyler?

26) What was King Richard II's role in the revolt?

27) Name three battles which were won by the English over the Hundred Years War.

28) Which city was attacked by the English in 1428, and which side won?

29) Which thirty year period saw the Wars of the Roses?

30) Which two houses were fighting during the Wars of the Roses? Describe their emblems.

31) Which three marriages did Henry VII arrange to stabilise England?

32) Give one other way in which Henry VII tried to stabilise the country during his reign.

Section Two
Tudors and Stuarts

	1509 — Henry VIII becomes King. He has six wives, but not at the same time.
Henry VIII makes himself Head of the Church of England, breaking away from the Roman Catholic Church. — **1534**	
Henry VIII starts to attack the monasteries, confiscating their valuables and land. — **1536**	
	1547 — Edward VI becomes King. He's sympathetic to Protestants. He's just a kid though, so his advisers have most of the power.
A new Book of Common Prayer is introduced. It is written in English, not Latin (a sign that it's fairly Protestant and untraditional). — **1549**	
	1553 — Mary I becomes Queen. She's strongly Catholic and reverses the religious reforms of Henry VIII and Edward VI.
	1558 — Elizabeth I becomes Queen. She's a bit cleverer than Mary. She has a really long reign until 1603, but never marries.
Elizabeth I tries to change the Church of England so both Catholics and Protestants will like it. — **1559**	
Mary Queen of Scots is executed. She was linked to Catholic plots to kill Elizabeth. — **1587**	
The Spanish send an Armada of ships against England. It is defeated. Hurrah. — **1588**	
	1603 — Elizabeth I dies childless. James Stuart (Mary Queen of Scots's son), already King of Scotland, becomes the new King of England.
	1625 — Charles I becomes King. He annoys a lot of people with expensive wars and high taxes.
Civil War begins in England. It's a fight between Royalists loyal to Charles I and Parliamentarians who want to get rid of the monarchy. — **1642**	
The Parliamentarians win the Civil War. They set up a republic called "The Commonwealth". Oliver Cromwell is their leader. — **1648**	
	1649 — Charles I is executed.
	1653 — Cromwell makes himself "Lord Protector".
	1658 — Cromwell dies, and is replaced by his son.
	1660 — The monarchy is brought back — this is called the Restoration. Charles II becomes King, after promising to rule with Parliament.
	1685 — James II becomes King. He's a Catholic, and is unpopular with the Protestants.
	1688 — James II's Protestant daughter, Mary, and her husband, William of Orange, take over the throne. James II runs away to France. Protestants call this the 'Glorious Revolution'.
James II tries to get his throne back by raising an army of Catholic supporters in Ireland. But his army is badly beaten at the Battle of the Boyne. — **1690**	
	1702 — Mary's sister Anne becomes Queen.
The Act of Union unites England and Scotland. — **1707**	
	1714 — Anne dies childless. A distant German relation becomes King George I.
A Scottish rebellion against the Act of Union fails. — **1715**	
	1727 — George I dies. His son becomes King George II.
Another Scottish rebellion, led by Bonnie Prince Charlie, also fails. — **1745**	

Religion and Henry VIII

Religion was a hot political potato for the Tudor kings and queens. The big changes started when <u>Henry VIII</u> broke away from the Roman Catholic Church and put the <u>English Church</u> under <u>his control</u>.

Religion was Important because it was linked to Politics

1) <u>Today</u> people are mostly <u>free</u> to worship however they want.
   In the <u>1500s</u> it was different — religion was tied up with <u>politics</u>
   and there was very little <u>religious tolerance</u>.

2) Rulers wouldn't allow their subjects to follow other faiths.
   This was believed to be <u>disloyal</u> and <u>subversive</u>.

3) For example, Elizabeth I decided on a middle ground of very
   <u>mild Protestantism</u> and wanted <u>all</u> her subjects to follow it.
   People who continued to support other faiths were <u>punished</u>.

   The Jesuit (Catholic) priest Edmund Campion was executed as a traitor during Elizabeth's reign.

   Some extreme Protestants, called Puritans, wanted more reforms than Elizabeth was prepared to allow. John Stubbs had his hand cut off for printing a book that supported Puritanism.

Henry VIII broke Away from the Roman Catholic Church

1) Henry VIII followed the Catholic Church at first and
   was called <u>Defender of the Faith</u> by the Pope. But his
   Catholic wife <u>Catherine of Aragon</u> didn't give him a <u>son</u>.

2) Henry decided he wanted to marry <u>Anne Boleyn</u> instead,
   but the Pope in Rome wouldn't let him get divorced.

3) Henry was still basically Catholic, but he broke away
   from Rome and got rid of the Roman Catholic
   monasteries because:

- he wanted a <u>son</u> to follow him
- he fancied <u>Anne Boleyn</u>
- he was short of <u>money</u>
- he wanted the extra <u>power</u> of controlling the Church
- he could keep the <u>nobles happy</u> by giving them
  church lands.

Portrait of Catherine of Aragon.

Catherine was the widow of Henry's elder brother Arthur. To get out of his marriage, Henry used a Bible extract that says you can't marry your brother's widow.

Written Source — 1530

"If the Pope is unwilling, we are left to find a remedy elsewhere. Some remedies are extreme ones, but a sick man seeks relief in any way he can find." *This extract is taken from a letter Henry had his bishops send to the Pope. Basically he is threatening the Pope, saying that if the Pope doesn't give him a divorce then Henry will take drastic actions to sort the situation out.*

Religion and Henry VIII

Henry destroyed the power of the Catholic Church in England

How Henry split from the Roman Catholic Church

1532 Henry stopped all payments going
from the Church in England to Rome.

1533 His marriage to Catherine was annulled and he married Anne.

1534 Henry made himself Head of the Church in England
and the Act of Supremacy made this official.

1536 He attacked the Catholic monasteries
and took their valuables and land.

1539 The Bible was translated into English. The Act of Six Articles
was passed, making the Church of England's beliefs more Catholic.

Henry had all the monks thrown out of the monasteries, and in many cases the buildings were then burnt or destroyed.

Problems were Caused by breaking away from Rome

1) Many Catholics still felt loyal to the Pope.

2) People resented the nobles getting the Church
lands and wealth.

3) Catherine of Aragon was the aunt of Charles V — one of
the most powerful rulers in Europe. Henry was creating a
powerful enemy by annulling his marriage to Catherine.

4) When the monasteries were dissolved poor people
lost a source of charity.

5) The dissolution of the monasteries provoked the
Pilgrimage of Grace — a revolt of 40,000 people
in the north of England.

6) The break away from Rome encouraged Protestants
to quarrel more with the Catholic Church.

© Hulton Archive/Getty Images

Portrait of King Henry VIII in 1540.

Henry made himself head of the Church in England...

Tudor religion is complicated. As a brief reminder — Henry VIII broke away from the Pope
but was still Catholic. He just wanted to have control over the Church so he could do
whatever the heck he wanted.

The Reformation and Edward VI

All the religious changes in England weren't happening in a vacuum — there were major religious arguments and changes going on in Europe as well.

The Reformation was happening in Europe

1) In the 1500s people in Northern Europe started getting seriously annoyed with corruption and superstition in the Roman Catholic Church.

2) Religious thinkers like Martin Luther (a German friar) and John Calvin (a French priest) wrote books and articles protesting about the state of the Catholic Church.

3) Protestants like Calvin and Luther wanted to reform Christian religion and make it easier for ordinary people to understand — e.g. by translating the Bible from Latin so ordinary people could understand it.

4) To the Catholic Church, Protestants were heretics. Some were executed, though the famous ones like Luther and Calvin survived.

Heretics were people whose beliefs didn't conform with the beliefs of the Catholic Church. Lots of people who were called heretics, like Protestants, still thought of themselves as Christians. Heresy weakened the Catholic Church and was considered a great sin, so many heretics were persecuted.

Edward VI was a Protestant

Henry VIII died in 1547 and his 9-year old son Edward became King. Edward had been brought up by a Protestant. Most English people were still Catholics, but Edward supported Protestants by:

1) saying that priests could marry (Catholic priests couldn't).

2) introducing a new Book of Common Prayer in 1549, written in English.

3) passing the Act of Uniformity to make everyone use the new Book of Common Prayer.

4) making services simpler and churches barer, in the Protestant fashion.

Portrait of Edward VI.

Written Source — 1547

"I trusted that you would have allowed me your poor sister to have the traditional Mass, which the King, your father and mine, with all his predecessors had." Part of a letter Princess Mary sent to Edward in 1547 begging him to let her receive a Catholic Mass. Edward wouldn't even let his sister Mary practise being a Catholic.

Mary I and Elizabeth I

Mary I was a strict Catholic

Edward died young in 1553. His sister Mary became Queen and ruled until her death in 1558. She was strongly Catholic and tried to reverse the religious changes of the previous reigns.

Portrait of Queen Mary.

1) She got rid of the Prayer books and the Act of Uniformity.

2) She restored the rule of the Pope over the Church in England in 1554 and married the Catholic Philip II of Spain.

3) She had about 300 Protestants burnt — including famous churchmen like Cranmer, Latimer, and Ridley. This led her to be labelled 'Bloody Mary' by Protestants like John Foxe.

4) During Mary's reign the Counter-Reformation was happening in Europe — the Catholic Church was declaring its power and dealing out very harsh punishments to Protestants.

> We know about many of the people who died for their religion because of a book by John Foxe, called Foxe's Book of Martyrs.

Elizabeth I tried to create a Moderate religious policy

1) Elizabeth I (1558-1603) tried to allow both Catholics and Protestants to worship — all under the official structure of the Church of England. As long as people went to church she didn't ask too much about what they believed.

2) She called herself Governor of the Church of England, rather than Head, by an Act of Supremacy (1559). A new Act of Uniformity (1559) insisted that everybody used a new prayer book. It was worded in a way that wouldn't offend Catholics too much.

3) As time passed, there were threats to her life from Catholics and she became harsher in her treatment of them. Catholics found themselves having to worship in secret.

> The Puritans were extreme Protestants who thought hard work and worship were really important. They strongly opposed frivolous things like theatre, dancing and alcohol.

© DEA PICTURE LIBRARY/Getty Images

Portrait of Queen Elizabeth I.

There's nothing like a bit of sibling rivalry...

Mary never liked Elizabeth — after all, Henry dumped Mary's mum for Elizabeth's mum. But as she had no children Mary had no choice but to make Elizabeth her heir. Elizabeth went on to be a better and more successful queen than Mary.

SECTION TWO — TUDORS AND STUARTS, BRITAIN 1509-1745

Mary Queen of Scots

It's not nice when some of your biggest problems come from your own family. Mary Queen of Scots was a real problem for Elizabeth, and they were cousins.

Mary and Elizabeth were Related

1) Mary's dad was James V of Scotland, one of Elizabeth's cousins.
2) This meant that Mary was a direct descendant of Henry VII — just like Elizabeth.
3) Mary became Queen of Scotland when she was six days old. She later married the French Dauphin (heir to the king), but then returned to Scotland when her husband died in 1561.

Scotland was Protestant but Mary was Catholic

1) By 1561, Protestant leaders like John Knox had become powerful in Scotland.
2) As a Catholic, Mary was treated with suspicion by many of her subjects.
3) Mary married Lord Darnley. It wasn't a very happy marriage, and Mary became very close to her advisor, the Earl of Bothwell. Mary and Darnley had a son, James.
4) In 1567, Darnley was murdered. Mary then (foolishly) married the Earl of Bothwell (the prime suspect and an unpopular man) just three months later.
5) The Scottish nobles turned against Mary. They exiled Bothwell and imprisoned her, making her infant son king instead.
6) Mary escaped and fled to England to ask for Elizabeth's help.

Portrait of Mary Queen of Scots.

Elizabeth had Mary Queen of Scots Executed

1) Elizabeth had Mary imprisoned because she was a potential threat to the throne.
2) Catholics who wanted to get rid of Elizabeth planned to put Mary on the throne. Elizabeth didn't punish Mary because she wasn't involved in the plans, and she was family.
3) Then Mary made a big mistake by writing to someone who was planning to kill Elizabeth. The letters were intercepted, and Mary was put on trial for treason.
4) Elizabeth was reluctant to kill Mary, but realised she would always be a threat. Eventually she signed the death warrant, and Mary was executed in 1587.

Elizabeth I — you wouldn't want to get into her bad books...

Mary Queen of Scots is seen as being a very glamorous character and loads of books and films have been made about her. But she was also vain, demanding and often selfish.

SECTION TWO — TUDORS AND STUARTS, BRITAIN 1509-1745

Relations with Other Countries

Elizabeth had a pretty stressful time with foreign nations, both in the British Isles and abroad.

Scotland's Friendship with France worried Elizabeth

1) Scotland had a long-standing alliance with France. Elizabeth worried that French troops would use Scotland as a passage into England.

2) The French Catholics had a large influence in Scotland, but this was unpopular with the Protestant nobles. In 1560, Elizabeth sent troops to support the Protestants. French forces withdrew from Scotland later that year.

3) James VI, Mary Queen of Scots' son, worked at a good relationship with Elizabeth. From the 1580s, Scotland and England became allies, and James succeeded Elizabeth peacefully when she died, becoming James I of England.

Portrait of James I of England.

There were several Irish Rebellions during her reign

1) Ireland was a problem for Elizabeth. Some Irish people were happy to be ruled by the English, but in others there were powerful clans who opposed it.

2) She gave her own lords lands in Ireland, hoping they would help her to regain some control, but some of them ignored her wishes.

3) There were three big rebellions against English rule during her reign. One, the Nine Years War, lasted from 1594-1603. Elizabeth was brutal in her tactics, burning whole villages to destroy the rebels.

4) In the end, a peace treaty was signed just after her death in 1603.

Relations between England and Spain got worse

Philip II (the King of Spain) got on well with Elizabeth to begin with, and even asked to marry her. But relations between the two countries gradually got worse.

1) Philip had been married to the English queen Mary, and he wanted his power in England back.

2) Many people in Catholic Spain thought that the Protestant Elizabeth should not be on the throne.

3) Elizabeth was concerned about Spanish support for Irish rebellions.

4) Elizabeth had been secretly encouraging attacks on Spanish ships.

5) Elizabeth had been helping Spain's enemies in the Netherlands.

6) In 1587, she executed Mary Queen of Scots — a Catholic queen.

The Armada

Elizabeth managed to defeat the Spanish army before they had ever set foot on English soil.

The **Spanish Armada** was **Defeated**

In May 1588 Philip sent the <u>Spanish Armada</u> (a fleet of boats) against England.
Within a few weeks what was left of the fleet was limping home, by escaping round the top
of Britain and back past Ireland. It was a <u>disaster</u> because —

1) The leader of the Armada, Medina Sidonia, was a <u>soldier</u> rather than a sailor.

2) The English had <u>faster ships</u> and <u>better sailors</u>.

3) The <u>Spanish soldiers</u> who were supposed to meet up with the Armada <u>couldn't get there</u>.

4) The English had crippled the Spanish fleet while it was in Calais harbour by sending in <u>fire ships</u>.

5) The Armada hadn't planned to sail all the way round Britain, but they were <u>forced to escape</u> that way. Ships were destroyed on rocks.

This Elizabethan playing card shows the defeat of the Spanish Armada by Sir Francis Drake and the British Navy.

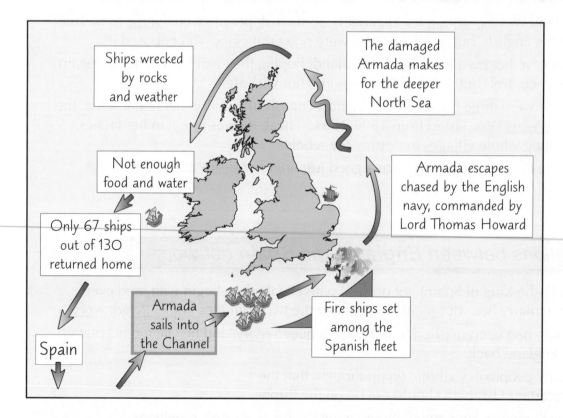

Written Source — 1588

"I know I have the body of a weak and feeble woman, but I have the heart and stomach of a king, and a king of England too, and think foul scorn that Parma or Spain, or any prince of Europe should dare to invade the borders of my realm... I myself will be your general, judge, and rewarder." *Elizabeth's speech to her army at Tilbury in 1588, before they attacked the Spanish.*

Sources and Questions

The Tudor monarchs sure liked stirring up a bit of trouble. Here are some source-based questions on the Tudors for you to answer. Remember, even when you're using modern sources you still need to think about whether they are biased.

1 *Elizabeth I had to deal with religious problems during her reign. These problems began earlier, in Henry VIII's reign. Read Sources A and B, then answer the questions below.*

> **Source A — J. Scott, a modern historian**
>
> In most villages the only large building, apart from the manor house, was the church. Everybody used the church, and not just for baptisms, marriages, funerals and services on Sundays. If there was a school, it was in the church. The church organised help for the poor. It was the centre of the village community.

> **Source B — R. J. Unstead, a modern historian**
>
> The Pope, who lived in Rome, was head of the Catholic Church, and all Kings and Princes were subject to him. Henry VIII wished to divorce his wife, Catherine of Aragon, so he could marry Anne Boleyn. The Pope would not allow him to do so and they quarrelled. Henry disobeyed the Pope and married Anne. He ordered the monasteries to be pulled down and seized all their land and riches.

a) Using Source A, explain why the Church was important to people in the 1500s.

b) Why did Henry VIII quarrel with the Pope according to Source B?

c) Say whether the following statement is true or false, and explain why.

"Most people wouldn't have minded Henry VIII's changes to the Church — it wasn't central to their life."

2 *Early in her reign Elizabeth I was fairly tolerant of Catholics. After 1568 there were Catholic plots against her and she became harsher.*

> **Source A — Elizabeth's attitude to religion, described by a modern historian**
>
> Elizabeth's views were remarkably tolerant for the age in which she lived. She believed that Catholics and Protestants were part of the same faith. Throughout her reign, Elizabeth's main concern was the peace and stability of her realm.

> **Source B — John Gerard, a Catholic preacher during Elizabeth's reign**
>
> We went to the torture room in a kind of solemn procession, the attendants walking along with lighted candles. They put my wrists into iron gauntlets and ordered me to climb two or three wicker steps. My arms were lifted up and they left me hanging by my toes.

gauntlets = gloves

a) According to Source A, what was Queen Elizabeth I's main concern?

b) Source B describes how Catholics were treated harshly. Why might Elizabeth have believed this would help bring peace and stability to England?

Sources and Questions

3 *In 1586, Elizabeth I's spies intercepted letters sent from Mary, Queen of Scots, to men planning to kill Elizabeth and make Mary Queen of England. Mary was charged with treason.*

Source A — Letter from Elizabeth I to Mary, Queen of Scots, 1586

You have in various ways and manners attempted to take my life and to bring my kingdom to destruction by bloodshed. I have never proceeded so harshly against you, but have, on the contrary, protected and maintained you like myself. I therefore require, charge, and command that you make answer, for I have been well informed of your arrogance.

Source B — The execution of Mary, Queen of Scots, from an eyewitness

Mary's two women, seeing her, were very upset, and crying and crossing themselves and praying in Latin. She, turning herself to them, embracing them...told them to pray for her and rejoice and not weep, for now they should see an end of all their mistress's troubles.

a) What does Source A suggest about how Elizabeth felt towards Mary?
   i) that Mary was a villain   ii) that Mary had betrayed her   iii) that Mary was innocent
b) According to Source B, how did Mary behave at her execution?
   Explain your answer using examples from Source B.

4 *Elizabeth had a troublesome relationship with Ireland during her reign. The most significant rebellion against English rule in Ireland was the Nine Years War, 1594-1603.*

Source A — An Irishman writes about Elizabeth in 1621

The kingdom [Ireland] blazed, burned, and perished with war, slaughter and famine... The tyrant, Queen Elizabeth, ordered that all should entirely abandon the Catholic faith, forsake the priests and accept the teachings and doctrines of heretic ministers. And to this they were compelled by fear, terror, punishment and violence.

Source B — William Saxby, Elizabeth's Chief Justice of Munster, describes the tactics of the Irish rebels, 1598.

Some have their throats cut, but not killed, some with their tongues cut out of their heads, others with their noses cut off... Those who yesterday were fed and nourished by the English, are now the thieves that violently take from them their corn, cattle and other goods.

a) Using Source A, which of these statements is the most accurate?
   i)   Elizabeth's policy in Ireland was peaceful, and had nothing to do with religion.
   ii) Elizabeth's policy in Ireland was often violent, but had nothing to do with religion.
   iii) Elizabeth's policy in Ireland was often violent, and had a lot to do with religion.
b) What does Source B suggest about the Irish as a people? Why might the author want to present them in this way?

Sources and Questions

5 *Elizabeth I never married. When she was young there was loads of discussion about who would be a good husband for her. Read the sources below and then answer the questions.*

Source A — A modern historian describes the issue of marriage for Elizabeth

From the moment Elizabeth became Queen, there was one question everyone was asking — who will the Queen marry? It was assumed that one of the first things the Queen would do would be to select a husband to help her govern her realm, and more importantly, to get her pregnant.

Source B — Philip II of Spain

consort = husband of a queen or wife of a king

It would be better for Elizabeth and her kingdom if she would take a consort who might relieve her of those labours that are only fit for men.

labours = tasks

a) Give two reasons why Elizabeth was expected to marry, according to Source A.

b) What do you think Philip of Spain means by "labours that are only fit for men" in Source B?

c) Do you think Philip's statement about Elizabeth in Source B is:

   i) fact

   ii) rumour

   iii) opinion

6 *Relations between England and Spain got worse and worse during Elizabeth's reign. In 1588 the Spanish sent an Armada of ships to fight the English. Read the sources and then answer the questions.*

Source A — An eyewitness account of the Spanish Armada

After the fierce battle we had off Calais on 8th August, continuing from morning until seven o'clock in the evening, which was our last day's fight, while our Armada was withdrawing — ah, it grieves me to recall it! — the enemy fleet pursued to harry us from their country.

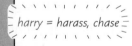
harry = harass, chase

Source B — An eyewitness account of the Spanish Armada

All that day we had with them a long and great fight. Everyone fought with great valour. In this fight there was some hurt done amongst the Spaniards. Our ships, God be thanked, have received little hurt and are of great force.

valour = courage

a) Do you think the author of Source A is English or Spanish? Explain your answer.

b) Do you think the author of Source B is English or Spanish? Explain your answer.

Charles I

In the 1600s things got tense between <u>Crown</u> (the King) and <u>Parliament</u>. The main quarrels were over <u>power</u>, the relationship between the monarchy and Parliament, and the <u>religion</u> of England.

Charles I (1625-49) made some **Unpopular Decisions**

1) Charles was responsible for <u>expensive wars</u> with France, Spain and Scotland. He also had to deal with rebellions in <u>Ireland</u>.

2) When Parliament refused to let him raise more taxes, Charles resorted to <u>illegal taxation</u> and tried to rule <u>without Parliament</u>.

3) Charles supported 'High Church' ceremonies and some people worried he wanted to make England <u>Catholic again</u>.

4) He made enemies by asking for <u>Ship Money</u> — a tax which was usually only collected when there was a war on.

5) Charles tried to do without Parliament for 11 years (1629-40). This finally led to <u>Civil War</u> in <u>1642</u> and led to <u>seven years</u> of struggle between <u>Royalists</u> and <u>Parliamentarians</u>.

Was **Charles I** a **Successful** monarch?

Whether you think Charles was a <u>good monarch</u> depends on what you think a good king <u>should</u> be like, e.g. if he should:

- Stay out of <u>debt</u>
- Have good relations with <u>Parliament</u>
- Stay out of arguments about <u>religion</u>
- Be successful in <u>war</u>.

Portrait of King Charles I.

© Hulton Archive/Getty Images

Charles messed up in all these areas —
- He had money problems
- He wanted to limit Parliament's power
- He caused uncertainty about religion
- He was beaten in war by the Scots.

Still, he was an old-fashioned monarch living in changing times. He thought he had a divine right to rule, with no need to share power with Parliament — just like in the old days.

Written Source — 1649

"Charles Stuart... had a wicked design to create an unlimited and tyrannical power, to rule according to his will, and to overthrow the rights and liberties of the people. He traitorously waged war against Parliament and the people... He is thus responsible for all the treasons, murders, rapings, burnings, damage and desolation caused during those wars. He is therefore, a tyrant, a traitor, and a murderer, and a public and implacable enemy to the Commonwealth." *The charges against Charles at his trial in 1649.*

The English Civil War

The Civil War was long and bloody and brought about many changes that can still be seen today — especially in our parliamentary system and the way the army is trained.

The **Civil War** was fought from **1642** to **1648**

Timeline of Cromwell and the Civil War

1641-2   Conflict between King and Parliament over war and taxes.

1642-8   Battles between Royalists and Parliamentarians.

1648   Charles I defeated by Cromwell's New Model Army at Preston.

England became known as "The Commonwealth", with Cromwell as President (there's more about Cromwell on p. 58).

1649   Charles I tried for treason and executed.

1651   Cromwell crushes attempt to get throne by Charles I's son, Charles II.

1658   Cromwell dies.

1660   Monarchy restored. Charles II becomes the new King.

Portrait of Royalist soldiers.

Parliamentarians called the Royalists 'Cavaliers' after the Spanish word 'caballeros', which means armed horsemen.

Engraving of a Parliamentarian soldier.

Royalists called the Parliamentarians 'Roundheads' because of the close-cropped heads of apprentices from London who supported Parliament.

Charles I — bad king or voice of God?

Charles had a very rocky relationship with Parliament. They wanted more power — but Charles reckoned he was "a little god" with a divine right to rule, and he didn't want to share power.

Causes of the Civil War

The Civil War was horrible. Some families ended up fighting each other, and civilians who didn't want to be involved had fighting in their towns and soldiers raiding their property.

There are different *Explanations* of *Why* the *War Started*

Religious Factors

Puritans wanted religious reform and were worried Charles had Catholic sympathies. He probably did — he tried to impose more elaborate services in church. He also married Henrietta Maria, a French Catholic, which worried lots of Protestants.

Political Factors

1) Parliament wanted to have more power, but Charles didn't want it to.
2) Charles attempted to rule without Parliament throughout the 1630s.
3) Parliament took control of the army in 1642 to stop Charles sending them to fight a war in Ireland that Parliament hadn't approved — this left Charles virtually powerless.

Economic Factors

1) Charles was spending more money than he collected in taxes.
2) Illegal methods of taxation were introduced and old methods were revived. Overall, people were paying a lot more tax.
3) The illegal taxes angered landowners and merchants, who complained to their MPs — this made Parliament even more angry with Charles.

Social Factors

1) The population of England was growing quickly — contributing to poverty and unemployment.
2) There were tensions between social classes — the middle classes getting richer, the nobility declining.

Written Source — 1654

"In every government there must be...[something] like a Magna Carta, which should be standing, unalterable... That Parliaments should not make themselves perpetual is fundamental." *Part of Cromwell's speech to the first Protectorate Parliament, September 1654. Cromwell was saying that it was important that there are always basic laws to protect people, but that it was also important that Parliament shouldn't always be made up of the same people.*

Causes of the Civil War

Some Historians blame Long-Term factors

Some <u>traditional</u> historians blame <u>long-term factors</u> for causing the Civil War —

1) Some historians say some of the problems went back to the reign of <u>James I</u> — he was unpopular with Parliament and they disagreed about <u>religion</u> and <u>finance</u>. James I really believed he ruled by <u>divine right</u> — an idea he passed on to his son Charles.

2) Class and other <u>social tensions</u> had been developing since the reign of Queen <u>Elizabeth I</u>.

Other Historians blame Short-Term factors

A more <u>recent</u>, <u>revisionist view</u> of historians is that <u>short-term factors</u> were more to blame. These short-term factors are shown in the box below.

Build up to the Civil War	
1630s	Proposed religious reforms angered Puritans.
1639 and 1640	England was defeated by Scotland in the religious Bishops' Wars.
1640	Charles called a Parliament in 1640. MPs began to demand political and religious reforms.
January 1642	Charles tried to arrest five MPs by taking 400 soldiers into the House of Commons. They escaped.
March 1642	Rebellion in Ireland, but Parliament didn't want to let Charles have an army to crush the rebellion — it would give him lots of power.
June 1642	Parliament passed the 19 propositions that demanded an increase in Parliament's power. Charles was angry and both sides raised armies.

© Mary Evans Picture Library

Charles I tried to arrest five MPs.

Charles tried to arrest the five MPs who led a rebellion against him in Parliament. However, they had been warned about Charles's plan so they escaped on boats down the River Thames.

It's all about points of view...

Historians criticise older historians' work and come up with new theories. So when you study a historical event there's usually a traditional view and a revisionist view about what happened.

Major Events of the Civil War

There were two phases to the Civil War — 1642-1646 and 1647-1649.
By the second phase the Parliamentarians were starting to win — their
<u>New Model Army</u> was really tough and disciplined.

The **Major Events** in the Civil War

1642 to 1646

August 1642	Charles raised an army in Nottingham, while Parliament raised its army in London.
October 1642	Battle at Edgehill, but no clear result.
1643	Many battles, including Newbury, but still no clear outcome.
June, July 1645	Parliament used the New Model Army to win important victories at Naseby and Langport.
1646	Charles fled to Scotland where he was captured and sold back to Parliament.

1647 to 1649

1647	Charles rejected a deal to give Parliament control of the army for 10 years and to allow freedom of worship. He <u>escaped</u> from prison and made a new deal with the <u>Scots</u>.
Summer 1648	The Royalists had <u>victories</u> in the North but were <u>defeated</u> by Cromwell and the New Model Army at <u>Preston</u>.
January 1649	The House of Commons set up a <u>high court of justice</u> and although Charles thought the court was illegal it found him guilty and sentenced him to <u>death</u>.

Parliament's Charges Against Charles:

- 'Wicked design' to create unlimited and tyrannical power.
- Tried to overthrow the rights and liberties of the people.
- Fought a traitorous war against Parliament and people.
- Responsible for treasons, rapes, burnings and damage of war.

Written Source — 1642

"Brother, what I feared is true — you are against the king. It breaks my heart to think that my father and I, who love you so dearly, should be your enemy because of our duty to the king. I am so troubled that I can write no more." *Part of a letter Edmund Verney sent to his brother Ralph in 1642. The brothers chose to fight for opposite sides in the Civil War.*

Major Events of the Civil War

The Civil War *Divided Families*

1) <u>Parliamentarian support</u> was strongest in the South and East. The main support for Parliament came from <u>small farmers</u>, <u>merchants</u> and <u>townspeople</u>.

2) <u>Royalist support</u> was strongest in the North, the West and in Wales. A greater majority of the <u>nobility</u> and the <u>gentry</u> supported the King rather than Parliament.

3) <u>Religion</u> was the most important factor in deciding which side people took. <u>Parliament</u> could count on the support of <u>English Puritans</u>. <u>Catholics</u> and <u>less radical Protestants</u> supported <u>Charles</u>.

4) It wasn't unusual for <u>families</u> to be <u>split</u> in their support for King or Parliament.

Charles had friends, but *Parliament* had *Money*

Although the Royalists had good generals, had brave troops and were skilled horsemen, <u>Parliament won</u>. Here's why:

1) Parliament had <u>skilled generals</u> like Fairfax and Cromwell.

2) It had the well organised, trained and disciplined <u>New Model Army</u>.

3) It had <u>control</u> of the <u>Navy</u> and was able to block French supplies to Charles.

4) It was able to use <u>taxes</u> to finance itself, while the King had to rely on friends and supporters.

5) <u>Charles</u> proved to be a <u>poor leader</u> and made bad tactical decisions.

Charles was beheaded on 30 January 1649 in front of Whitehall in London.

It is believed that Charles wore really thick underclothes so he wouldn't get cold — he was worried that if he got cold he would shiver and the crowd would think he was scared.

© Hulton Archive / Getty Images

Charles I being executed.

It always seems to come down to religion...

Although the Civil War was basically King against Parliament, religion was still a major issue. Religion was really political in 1600s England — it influenced which side people fought on in the war.

England After the Civil War

King Charles had gone, but the arguments about what should replace him were only just beginning. The period between Charles I and Charles II is called the 'interregnum' — the period between reigns.

There were *Different Ideas* about how to *Run the Country*

The winners soon began to argue amongst themselves. Different groups had different ideas about how the country should be run.

1) Republicans were happy to see Parliament continue to rule. It wasn't a full Parliament though — MPs who supported the King and all of the House of Lords were excluded. It was called the Rump Parliament.

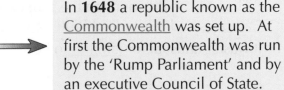

In **1648** a republic known as the Commonwealth was set up. At first the Commonwealth was run by the 'Rump Parliament' and by an executive Council of State. Oliver Cromwell was President.

2) Royalists looked forward to the return of the monarchy, hopefully in the shape of Charles I's son, who fled abroad after his defeat in 1651 (see p. 51).

3) The army, especially the generals, wanted to keep the power and influence they had during the Civil Wars.

Some groups wanted *Social* and *Economic Equality*

1) The Levellers were Puritans. They wanted to abolish the monarchy and the privileges of the nobles. When the Levellers tried to build support in the army, Cromwell moved quickly to crush them.

2) The Diggers were a religious and social movement who wanted to farm wastelands for poor people's benefit. When the Diggers planted on common land at St George's Hill in Surrey their efforts were quickly destroyed by a local mob.

There was a *Struggle for Power* 1649-1653

1) Cromwell strengthened his position as President of the Council of State by crushing revolts in Ireland and Scotland (see p. 57) and defeating Charles II.

2) After a clash with the Rump Parliament, Cromwell replaced it with a Nominated Assembly in 1653. It passed 29 measures dealing with legal and religious issues.

3) There were some moderates (people who oppose extreme opinions) in Parliament who felt the Assembly was too radical.

4) Moderates and the army produced an "Instrument of Government" that named Cromwell as Protector for life (King in all but name) in 1657.

5) Tension between civilian politicians and army leaders increased. MPs wanted less religious tolerance, fewer powers for the army and a strengthened Parliament.

Parliament was unable to make its mind up...

Maybe England wasn't ready for a republic and completely new form of government. No sooner had they killed Charles than they were trying to make Cromwell as much like a king as possible.

Revolts in Ireland and Scotland

The troubles in England were nothing compared to the problems that Parliament had to deal with in Ireland and Scotland — where there were full scale Royalist rebellions.

The **Irish** wanted to put a **Catholic King** on the throne

The Irish wanted to make Charles II (the son of executed king Charles I) king. A rebellion began.

1) Cromwell was asked by parliament to bring Ireland under English control and confiscate land from rebels (who were mainly Irish Catholics).

2) He captured the town of Drogheda in 1649, killing many of the inhabitants and captured soldiers. He also took Wexford, killing people who refused to surrender.

3) Many towns then surrendered, and Cromwell spared the people.

4) Catholic lands went to Protestants, including Cromwell's soldiers. Many Irish people were banished to the West of Ireland. Catholicism was forbidden.

Cromwell and his army attacking Drogheda.

The **Rebellion** moved into **Scotland**

1) Charles (the son of Charles I) was proclaimed King of Scotland in 1649.

2) Charles landed in Scotland in June 1650. He made a deal with the Protestant 'Covenanters' to get their support.

3) Oliver Cromwell led an English army into Scotland. He defeated the Scots at the Battle of Dunbar in 1650.

4) This weakened the Scots. Charles decided to invade England, but was defeated at the Battle of Worcester in 1651.

5) Charles escaped to France. Large parts of Scotland came under English control.

People **Argue** about whether Cromwell was **Too Cruel**

A tricky subject this one — some people say he was just doing his job and was no worse than any other leader, some think he was a mass murderer. There are arguments on both sides...

Cromwell was too cruel...	Cromwell wasn't that bad...
The massacres at Drogheda and Wexford have never been forgiven. Many say he was less merciful than he could have been — thousands of Irish Catholics were killed or lost their land.	Cromwell ordered that civilians should not generally be harmed. He offered towns the chance to surrender. It wasn't unusual in this period of history to kill those that opposed you, even if they were unarmed civilians. When towns surrendered, he spared the inhabitants.

Written Source — 1649

"I believe we put to the sword the whole number of defendants. I do not think 30 of them escaped. Those that did are in safe custody waiting to be sent to the Barbadoes. I am persuaded this is the righteous judgement of God..." *Cromwell's description of the Battle of Drogheda, part of a letter he wrote on 16 September 1649.*

Oliver Cromwell

Oliver Cromwell was a puritan MP (Member of Parliament) — he was really religious and believed God supported all his actions. He became powerful as a Parliamentarian general and ended up leading the country as Lord Protector.

Views of Cromwell — Was he a **Protector** or **Dictator**?

Cromwell as Protector

1) Religious tolerance for Protestants was established.
2) Jews were allowed to return to England.
3) Important naval reforms were introduced.
4) He made good decisions when dealing with foreign countries.

Cromwell as Dictator

1) The Protectorate was basically Cromwell's personal, Puritan rule.
2) He sacked Parliament for criticising his religious policies.
3) Taxes were collected without Parliament's consent.
4) Judges who ruled against him were sacked.
5) In 1656 some MPs asked Cromwell to take the title of King.
   Cromwell knew the army was against the title of King.
   He dismissed Parliament and got the army to collect taxes instead.
6) People who were against Cromwell (dissenters) were crushed,
   often brutally, e.g. in Ireland and Scotland.

Engraving of Oliver Cromwell.

Cromwell's life	
1599	Born in Huntingdon
1616	Cambridge University
1640	Becomes an MP
1642-48	Rises through ranks of Parliamentary Army
1649	Supports trial and execution of King Charles
1653	Becomes Lord Protector
1658	Dies, 3rd September
1661	Dug up and 'executed' by Royalists

Written Source — 1658

"You drew me here to accept the place I now stand in. There is ne'er a man within these walls that can say, "Sir, you sought it", nay, not a man nor woman treading upon English ground."
Cromwell's speech to Parliament in February 1658. He is basically saying that he never set out to replace the King and become Lord Protector, but that it was the will of God and Parliament.

After Cromwell

Cromwell proved to be a strong leader and a king in everything but name. When he died Parliament wanted another iconic figure to lead them.

The **Monarchy** was **Restored** in 1660

Cromwell had said that his son should be the next Lord Protector — as if he was a king passing on power to his heir. After Cromwell died, his son Richard ruled briefly and unsuccessfully. Richard was a farmer and not that good at ruling. Meanwhile, Charles II was living in exile on the continent.

1) Parliament decided to ask Charles to return to England and become king.

2) In April 1660 Charles made the 'Declaration of Breda', promising to rule with Parliament and not punish his enemies if he was made King.

3) English politicians invited Charles II to be king. The return of the monarchy is called the Restoration.

4) Those who had signed Charles I's death warrant were executed and strict anti-Puritan laws were passed — this broke the promises made at Breda.

5) Anti-Catholic laws were abolished, although Parliament forced the new King to accept an anti-Catholic act in 1673.

When Cromwell died he was given a massive, expensive funeral in London.

Soon after Charles II came to the throne Cromwell's body was dug up, hanged and his head was stuck on a pole.

Charles was King when the Bubonic Plague hit London in 1665. The following year his luck didn't get any better as the Great Fire of London destroyed lots of the city.

How much **Changed** because of the **Civil Wars**?

1) The monarchy was restored — England didn't stay a republic for long.

2) The Protestant Anglican Church of the interregnum didn't survive the restoration of the monarchy.

3) Puritans lost many of their civil and political rights after the restoration.

4) The Glorious Revolution of 1688 (which settled the nature of the relationship between Crown and Parliament) might not have happened without the earlier experiences of Civil War and Protectorate.

Dictator or Protector — you decide...

Oliver Cromwell won a civil war, overthrew a king and dismissed a Parliament — it's no wonder Richard couldn't live up to his dad's reputation.

Sources and Questions

Identifying the causes of historical events is really important when you study history.
When looking at sources you need to be aware that historians have to choose
events or issues they think are the causes — but there's not always a right answer.
Here are a few questions to get you thinking about the causes of some events.

1 *There was a Civil War in England in the 1640s. Historians disagree about its causes.
Read Sources A and B and answer the questions below.*

> **Source A — John Morrill, a modern historian**
>
> England in the 1630s was not a state sliding into civil war and
> anarchy. The early Stuart state saw fewer treason trials, no
> revolts, fewer riots. The civil wars grew out of the policies and
> out of the particular failings of a particular king, Charles I.

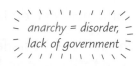

*anarchy = disorder,
lack of government*

> **Source B — Causes of the English Civil War by Conrad Russell
> (1990) By permission of Oxford University Press**
>
> The Civil War was the result of three long-term causes of instability,
> all of them well established before Charles came to the throne
> — the problem of multiple kingdoms, the problem of religious
> division, and the breakdown of a financial and political system.

a) Which of the sources blames Charles I's personality and leadership for causing the Civil War?

b) What evidence is there in Source A that the 1630s was a peaceful time?

c) Is the following statement true or false? Give reasons for your answer.

"Source B agrees with Source A. It says that short-term causes
were to blame for the English Civil War."

2 *Oliver Cromwell became Lord Protector in 1653, which made him the most powerful man
in England. He is a controversial figure — some historians think he ruled like a dictator.*

> **Source A — Timeline of events in Cromwell's career**
>
> 1653   Cromwell is made Lord Protector by Parliament.
>
> 1654   A new Parliament meets after MPs are forced to sign an agreement
> recognising Cromwell as Protector. If they don't sign it they have to resign.
>
> 1655   Cromwell dissolves Parliament angrily, after a dispute about
> religious policy.
>
> 1656   A new Parliament begins. 100 MPs are excluded from it.
>
> 1657   Parliament offers Cromwell a new constitution and the Crown of
> England. He accepts the constitution but not the Crown.

a) Write down two events from the timeline which support the idea that Cromwell behaved
like a dictator rather than a protector.

b) Write down one event which supports the idea that Oliver Cromwell did not want to
become king.

Sources and Questions

3 The Civil War was between Royalists who were loyal to King Charles I, and Parliamentarians who wanted Parliament to rule instead. Look at the sources and answer the questions below.

Source A — Map Showing England in 1642

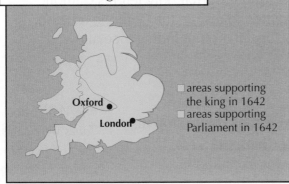

□ areas supporting the king in 1642
□ areas supporting Parliament in 1642

Oxford •
London •

Source B — Angus Stroud, a modern historian

Charles I was not always able to provide decisive leadership... Scottish intervention in the Civil War tipped the scales heavily in Parliament's favour...

There were able generals on the King's side, but key to the Parliamentarians' victory was the emergence of Sir Thomas Fairfax and Oliver Cromwell. The success of the New Model Army in 1645-6 owed much to the leadership of these two men.

able = good

... = if you see three dots, it means that part of the source has been left out.

Source C — A historian from the 1800s describes the Royalist Army

Upon the King's return from Oxford there appeared nothing but dejection of mind, discontent, and secret mutiny in the army. There was anger and jealousy amongst the officers, everyone accusing another of want of courage and conduct in the actions of the field.

want = lack

field = battle field

a) In 1642, which side (Parliamentarians or Royalists) had control of London and the South East of England?

b) Copy and complete the sentences below. Use Sources A-C to work out which words from the box below you need to fill the blanks.

The .... won the Civil War for a number of reasons.

<u>Reason 1</u> They controlled .... and the South East of England where there was a large population and more wealth than in other areas.

<u>Reason 2</u> The Royalist army was very .... and had low morale.

<u>Reason 3</u> Another country, ... , supported the Parliamentarian side.

<u>Reason 4</u> The Royalist leader was .... He was not a very good military leader. The Parliamentarians had better leaders like .... and ....

<u>Reason 5</u> The Parliamentarians were very well organised. Their army was called the ....

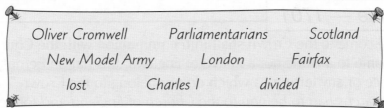

Oliver Cromwell   Parliamentarians   Scotland
New Model Army   London   Fairfax
lost   Charles I   divided

The Glorious Revolution

James II was King after Charles II. His Catholicism caused loads of problems. Britain's first political party — called the 'Whigs' — couldn't stand him and wanted a Protestant monarch instead.

The Catholic *James II* didn't have everyone's support

Charles II died in 1685 leaving no legitimate male children. That only left his Catholic brother James to follow him, as James II. James wanted to restore the Catholic religion. He gave Catholics important jobs and in 1688 his Declaration of Indulgence allowed Catholics to worship freely.

As a result —

1) Parliament split into two groups — Whigs, who didn't want James on the throne, and Tories, who didn't think it was their job to stop it.

2) The Duke of Monmouth (an illegitimate son of Charles II) decided to rebel. The rebellion failed and he was executed.

3) At first James had no kids so the Protestants reckoned they could put a Protestant on the throne after he died. But then James had a son.

The Whigs and the Tories were two of the first political parties in the world.

> In 1688 Protestants spread the story that James II's baby wasn't his, but had been smuggled into the palace hidden in a bed-warmer. James Edward Stuart was known as the Warming Pan Baby.

4) Some people asked James's Protestant daughter Mary and her husband William of Orange to take the throne. William of Orange came from part of what we now call Holland.

Reproductions of portraits of William and Mary, painted in the 17th century.

Written Source — 1701

"That whoever shall come to the Crown shall join communion with the Church of England. That if the Crown come to anyone not a native of England, this nation be not bound to engage in war for the defence of any territories which do not belong to the Crown." *Act of Settlement, 1701, meant all monarchs had to belong to the Church of England and foreign kings couldn't use the English army to defend their home country.*

The Glorious Revolution

William of Orange became William III of England

1) In <u>1688</u> William of Orange decided to sail to England to invade and <u>take the throne</u>.

2) James II lost his nerve and <u>escaped</u> to <u>France</u>, and the throne was offered to both William and Mary. William of Orange became <u>William III</u>.

3) There were still many <u>supporters</u> of James II living in Scotland, Ireland and France. James' supporters became known as <u>Jacobites</u> (Jacob is the Latin for <u>James</u>).

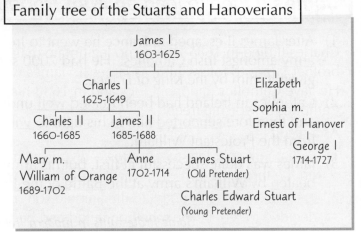

Family tree of the Stuarts and Hanoverians

James I
1603-1625

Charles I
1625-1649

Elizabeth

Sophia m.
Ernest of Hanover

Charles II
1660-1685

James II
1685-1688

George I
1714-1727

Mary m.
William of Orange
1689-1702

Anne
1702-1714

James Stuart
(Old Pretender)

Charles Edward Stuart
(Young Pretender)

The dates given here are the dates each monarch reigned.

The **Protestants** called this the **Glorious Revolution**

1) When William became King, the Protestants called it the <u>Glorious Revolution</u>.

2) <u>Catholics</u> didn't agree. They thought that the throne had been <u>stolen</u> from James and that he still had a right to it.

3) <u>Parliament</u> made sure that the new monarchs would not become too powerful and William had to agree to the <u>Bill of Rights</u> in 1689. In 1701 the <u>Act of Settlement</u> made Parliament even stronger and said the British monarch could never be Catholic, or even marry a Catholic.

4) This was the start of a <u>new kind</u> of monarchy — even though the monarch still had a lot of power, the people in <u>Parliament</u> had <u>more</u>.

The Bill of Rights limited the power of the monarchy. It meant that if any monarch didn't obey the rules they could be dismissed and replaced. By signing the Bill of Rights William and Mary agreed that:
- raising taxes without Parliament's permission was illegal.
- raising an army in peacetime without Parliament's permission was also illegal.
- there should be freedom of speech in Parliament.

It's a family affair...

You'll understand all this better if you study the <u>family tree</u> on this page. Spot the danger from the Catholic James Stuart waiting to take the throne. And a major problem for the Protestants is that William and Mary don't have <u>any children</u> to follow them.

Impact on Ireland

The Glorious Revolution was pretty inglorious in Ireland and Scotland. Many people in these areas were Catholic and supported James II. William of Orange defeated them — and it was very <u>bloody</u>.

James II tried to lead an Irish Rebellion

© Hulton Archive/Getty Images

Portrait of James II in 1670.

1) After <u>James II</u> escaped to France he went to <u>Ireland</u> to raise an <u>army</u> amongst Irish <u>Catholics</u>. He had 7000 soldiers with him, given to him by the King of France.

2) Catholics in Ireland had been <u>treated well</u> under James's rule and therefore <u>supported</u> him in his fight to <u>win back his throne</u> from the Protestant William.

3) James was quite successful at first, but his army was then badly <u>beaten</u> by William's army at the <u>Battle of the Boyne</u> in 1690.

Some Protestants in modern Ireland call themselves Orangemen and celebrate the anniversary of the Battle of the Boyne.

The impact of the Glorious Revolution on Ireland

The Catholics <u>lost ownership</u> of a lot of land during the Glorious Revolution.

1) In 1640 Catholics occupied 60% of Irish land.

2) By 1689 Catholics only occupied 20% of Irish land — the rest was in Protestant hands.

The <u>Treaty of Limerick</u> in <u>1691</u> allowed some religious freedom to Irish Catholics and gave back some of their land. However these promises were broken and Limerick became known as the "<u>City of the Broken Treaty</u>".

The Main Events of the Irish Rebellion

1688 — James II escaped to France. William and Mary took the throne.

1689 — James's army in Ireland attacked the Protestant city of Londonderry.

1690 — William's army took Belfast and beat James's troops at the Battle of the Boyne in June 1690. James escaped to France and never came back.

1691 — The Catholics finally lost the city of Limerick and had to admit defeat. Many Catholics had to give up their lands to Protestants who had supported William.

Orangemen's Day celebrates William's victory...

Although Orangemen celebrate William's victory at the Battle of the Boyne on 12th July, the battle actually took place on 1st July. This is because Britain was still using the old Julian calendar when the battle happened, but changed to using the Gregorian calendar (which we still use today) in 1752. This wiped 11 days out of the British calendar.

Impact on Scotland

The Catholic supporters of James II in Scotland weren't successful either.

The impact of the Glorious Revolution on **Scotland**

1) In Scotland, extreme <u>Protestants</u> called <u>Presbyterians</u> wanted the Glorious Revolution to go even further. Their Church system was called the <u>Kirk</u>.

2) <u>Catholic Highlanders</u> reacted differently — they supported the Catholic <u>James II</u> and were prepared to fight William of Orange.

3) At first things went <u>badly</u> for William in the <u>Highlands</u>. James's supporters, led by the 1st Viscount of Dundee, won the <u>Battle of Killiecrankie</u> in July 1689. But Dundee was <u>killed</u> at Killiecrankie and this weakened the Scottish forces.

Engraving by Noel Paton, a 19th century Scottish artist. It shows the Jacobites carrying Dundee's body from the battlefield at Killiecrankie.

4) The Highlanders were from different families (called <u>clans</u>) and there was some <u>infighting</u> — they <u>weren't</u> very well organised or <u>unified</u>. William bribed some of the Scottish chiefs to stop fighting him.

5) In 1692, supporters of William <u>massacred</u> one whole clan, the MacDonalds, while they slept at <u>Glencoe</u>. The MacDonalds had refused to support William. William's <u>opponents</u> were able to <u>use</u> this terrible news to make him even more <u>unpopular</u> in the north of Scotland. Even after William won there were still lots of <u>Jacobites</u> left in Scotland who didn't want him to be King.

Catholic rebellions were a problem for William...

William saw the Catholics as a major threat to his position as King, which is why he spent so much time fighting them. It wasn't just the Catholics in Ireland and Scotland he was afraid of, William was also worried about the French — the Catholic French King, Louis XIV, was trying to cause trouble for William at home so that William would be too busy to invade France.

England and Scotland United

In 1707 England joined with Scotland. The Scots weren't exactly thrilled but were bullied into it by England. There was a Jacobite rebellion against the English ruler in 1715 — but it failed.

England wanted to keep a **Protestant** ruler

1) Mary's sister Anne became queen in 1702. All of Anne's children died before she did. This was a big problem for Protestants who didn't want the Catholic James Edward Stuart (the Old Pretender) to claim the throne.

2) So when Anne died in 1714 the throne passed to a Protestant relation of Anne's who became George I. The royal family were now called Hanoverians (they came from Hanover in Germany). George couldn't speak much English and spent a lot of time in Germany. He was not very popular.

Reproduction of Kneller's portrait of George I.

© Mary Evans Picture Library

The **1707 Act of Union** united England and Scotland

Uniting Scotland and England was important for the English government. It would keep Scotland under control in case more trouble came from the Catholics. The Scots were forced to agree to union because the English threatened to stop trade between the two countries.

The Act of Union was passed in 1707. These were its main points —

1) Scotland couldn't have its own Parliament, but could send 45 members to the English Parliament and 16 lords to the English House of Lords.

2) Scotland could keep its own legal system.

3) Scotland would have to agree to Protestants always being on the throne.

4) Both countries could trade equally.

5) Both countries would use the same coins.

6) Scotland would have its own Church, called the Kirk.

7) Both countries would use the same flag.

> It was after this Act of Union that England, Scotland and Wales were referred to as "The United Kingdom of Great Britain".

Written Source — 1706

"For the English, the Union will make no change... But the Scots will have to pay the English debts, now and in the future. Scotland will lose the right to manage its own affairs. For the Scots, the Union will be a complete surrender." *Lord Belhaven's speech to the Scottish Parliament in 1706. He was arguing strongly against union with England.*

England and Scotland United

The 1715 Rebellion against the Act of Union failed

A lot of people in Scotland weren't keen on the Act of Union. They hated <u>paying taxes</u> to England and thought England was <u>interfering</u> too much in their way of life.

In <u>1715</u> <u>James Edward Stuart</u> finally made his move to take the throne. He and his supporters, the <u>Jacobites</u>, rebelled and invaded England.

The rebellion was a failure. James's forces were <u>poorly led</u> by the Earl of Mar and both men ended up <u>escaping</u> to France.

The <u>Jacobites lost</u> because —

1) The <u>French</u> couldn't help because they were busy fighting elsewhere.
2) Many Scots were getting <u>richer</u> through trade with England and didn't want to provoke harsh punishments.
3) Some Scots, especially Protestants in the <u>lowlands</u>, were getting used to English rule.
4) Some Scots didn't like James Edward Stuart's <u>links</u> with the French.
5) James had very <u>few supporters</u> in areas of the United Kingdom outside Scotland.
6) The <u>Jacobites</u> didn't always agree on what they wanted.
7) James <u>lacked confidence</u> that the rebellion would succeed.

James Edward Stuart (also known as The Old Pretender) and his council during the first Jacobite Rising.

Time to move on...

Having been defeated by two different English kings you might think that the Scots would give up, especially after having signed the Act of Union. But no, the Scots still had one last uprising left in them...

Bonnie Prince Charlie

Next upon the throne after George I was his son George II. The Jacobites were still a threat, especially in the Highlands of Scotland. In 1745 Bonnie Prince Charlie started a new Jacobite rising.

Bonnie Prince Charlie's *1745 Rising* was unsuccessful

By 1745 much of the British army was in Europe fighting — so the Jacobites took their chance. The 1745 Jacobite rising was led by Charles Edward Stuart, who was the son of James Edward Stuart (the Old Pretender). Charles was known as the Young Pretender or Bonnie Prince Charlie.

The Main Events of the 1745 Jacobite rising

1745	Charles landed in Scotland. Thousands of Highlanders joined him. By the end of the year they had taken Edinburgh and captured Carlisle. They advanced into England as far as Derby, hoping to gather support. They realised that they weren't strong enough and retreated to Scotland.
1746	English forces were being strengthened and were now led by the king's son, the cruel Duke of Cumberland. The Scots won the battle at Falkirk but many of Charles's army went home.
April 1746	The Scottish forces were savagely defeated at Culloden. Charles escaped to France.

After the defeat at Culloden, Charlie was a wanted man, with a reward of £30,000 offered for his capture. A woman called Flora MacDonald dressed him as her serving woman and took him to the Isle of Skye — and from there he escaped to France.

*As the grandson of James II, Bonnie Prince Charlie did have a legitimate claim to the throne.
But he wasn't Scottish or English, he was actually born in Rome and he spent most of his life living in Italy and France — where he was treated like a prince.*

© Hulton Archive/Getty Images

Portrait of Bonnie Prince Charlie.

Bonnie Prince Charlie never got to be called King...

Bonnie Prince Charlie was the grandson of King James II — the one who was deposed by William of Orange. Even after James II had been deposed the Pope still recognised him as King of England and Scotland, and the Pope went on to acknowledge James's son as the rightful King. But when it came to Charles, the Pope decided that he wouldn't be acknowledged as King.

Bonnie Prince Charlie

Charles **Didn't** get the **Support** he needed to win

The defeat of the rising ended the Jacobite threat to English power in Scotland.
The main reasons for the defeat of the Jacobite forces were —

1) The Jacobites needed help from France, and it didn't arrive.
2) Cumberland had ten of the best battalions and some troops from Holland.
3) Charles got no real support from the English or the lowlands of Scotland.
4) Charles was not a good military leader.
5) Many English people did not want another Catholic king.

"God save the King" became the new national anthem after Culloden, to celebrate the Hanoverian victory.

How united was the **United Kingdom**?

1) Wales had been largely controlled by 'March Lords', who were English but made their own laws and had private armies. In 1536, Henry VIII officially united England and Wales in what would become known as the first Act of Union (a second one was signed in 1543). This gave the king total control of Welsh law and eventually Wales itself.

2) Ireland was controlled by Protestants who were loyal to England (see p. 57). So after the Act of Union in 1707 joining Scotland to England, Britain was officially united.

3) But some people didn't think so. Catholics in Ireland hated the Protestant rulers. In Scotland, Cumberland was so cruel after Culloden that there was hatred of English rule in the Highlands.

4) On the other hand, some areas were learning to accept the new United Kingdom and many people in Scotland were becoming richer through trade with England.

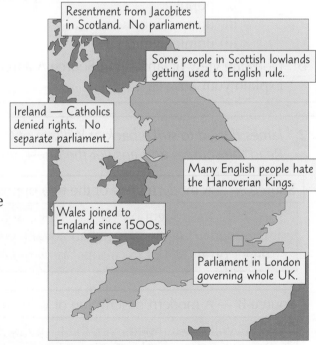

Resentment from Jacobites in Scotland. No parliament.

Some people in Scottish lowlands getting used to English rule.

Ireland — Catholics denied rights. No separate parliament.

Many English people hate the Hanoverian Kings.

Wales joined to England since 1500s.

Parliament in London governing whole UK.

There was no happy ending for Bonnie Prince Charlie...

Bonnie Prince Charlie may have been a good-looking guy in his youth, who led a failed rebellion and dressed up as a woman, but it all went downhill after that. He fled to France, his supporters abandoned him and he ended up an alcoholic.

Sources and Questions

Two key skills in history are to be able to understand the point a source is making and to be able to find the facts you need from a source. This set of questions will help you practise these skills.

1 *In 1688-89 William of Orange and his wife Mary took over the English throne from the unpopular King James II. This is known as the 'Glorious Revolution'.*

Source A — A modern view of James II

Unfortunately James II was not a successful King. For example, he was known to take offence if people didn't like his policies. He also insisted that monarchs had a divine right to rule, which was seen as old-fashioned. He tried to get the Church of England to return to the Pope and the Roman Catholic Church, and that wasn't popular either.

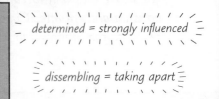

divine right = belief that a king could do whatever he wanted because he was chosen by God

Source B — The Bishop of Salisbury describes King James II

James II had no true judgement and was quickly determined by those whom he trusted... He was in favour of rougher methods. He continued, for many reasons, dissembling the Church of England.

determined = strongly influenced

dissembling = taking apart

a) Complete the following sentence by choosing one of options i)-iii).
   According to Source A, James II was...
      i) popular.
      ii) unsuccessful.
      iii) unintelligent.

b) Does the view of James II in Source A agree with the view of James II in Source B? Explain your answer.

2 *James II tried to strike back at William of Orange by leading a rebellion from Ireland. Read the sources and answer the questions which follow.*

Source A — A modern view of the two opposing sides at the Battle of the Boyne

The Battle was fought on 1st July 1690, at a formidable river bend four miles west of Drogheda. The two kings had advantages over one another. James had the stronger position, but his troops appeared to be inferior in quality and quantity.

Source B — A modern description of William's involvement in the Battle of the Boyne

When William slumped over, the Irish thought he had been killed. His men were quickly relieved when he said, "There is no harm done, but the bullet came quite close enough." His injury did not prevent him from spending nineteen hours in the saddle that day.

a) Complete the following sentence by choosing one of options i)-iii).
   Source A says that James' troops were...
      i) better trained and more numerous than William's.
      ii) less numerous and not as well trained as William's.
      iii) late for the battle.

b) What do you think the author of Source B wanted readers to think about William? Give reasons for your answer.

Sources and Questions

3   During Queen Anne's reign the 1707 Act of Union was passed, joining England and
Scotland. Read Sources A and B then answer the questions below.

Source A — A modern view of attitudes to the Union

The English attitude was that the only benefit in a United Kingdom was in Scotland's
favour. The Scots argument was that their more wealthy, more populated and more
powerful neighbours would just swallow up the Scottish nation.

Source B — A historian describes the effects of the Union

England made her money freely available to Scottish
MPs if they supported the Union. In the words of Robert
Burns, they were bought and sold for English gold.

a)   Why were the Scots against the Union, according to Source A?
b)   Which small group of Scots stood to gain from the Union according to Source B?

4   Charles Stuart, or 'Bonnie Prince Charlie', was the grandson of James II.
He and his father had a claim to the English and Scottish thrones.

Source A — The 1745 rebellion

In 1745, he [Charles Stuart] made his own
attempt to put his father on the throne.
He landed in Scotland with a handful of
men, raised an army and invaded England.

Source B — A historian describes Charles' later life

He became an alcoholic drifter. Even the Highland clans deserted him in the
end, irritated with his temper, his poor leadership, his lack of political tact... A
charismatic but supremely selfish man, he died where he was born, in Rome.

a)   Read Source A. Which pair of words best describe Charles Stuart in his early life?
i)   motivated and ambitious
ii)   lazy and unconcerned
iii) rich and bored
b)   Compare Sources A and B. According to the sources, how did
Charles Stuart's character change in later life?

SECTION TWO — TUDORS AND STUARTS, BRITAIN 1509-1745

Summary Questions

That was your whirlwind tour of 300-odd years of blood spattered uprisings and rebellions. Lots of stuff happened, but it shouldn't be confusing, not if you work through these questions. That way you can get everything clear in your head and go back and look up any stuff you don't know.

1) Is this true or false? "In the 1500s religion was separate from politics."
2) Give four reasons why Henry VIII wanted to break away from the Roman Catholic Church.
3) Write down one problem created by the dissolution of the monasteries.
4) Why did Mary Tudor become known as 'Bloody Mary'?
5) Which of the following sentences describes Elizabeth I's religious policy?
    a) A moderate policy — attempting to keep English Protestants and Catholics in one Church.
    b) An unrealistic policy — it tried to make Britons become Mormons.
6) What year was Mary Queen of Scots executed?
7) Why was Elizabeth I worried about Scotland's friendship with France?
8) What happened from 1594-1603?
9) Give three reasons why relations between England and Spain got worse during Elizabeth I's reign.
10) Was the Spanish Armada's attack on England in 1588 a success for Spain?
11) Write down three reasons why Charles was unpopular with parliament before the Civil War.
12) Briefly give one example for each of the following factors that helped cause the Civil War —
    a) religious factors   b) political factors   c) economic factors   d) social factors.
13) In what year was Charles I executed?
14) What was the 'Rump Parliament'?
15) What was the name of the new republic created in the British Isles in 1648?
16) Who were the Diggers?
17) Give one example of an Irish town where Cromwell killed the inhabitants.
18) Write down four ways in which Cromwell acted like a dictator.
19) What was the Restoration?
20) Why did the Whigs dislike James II?
21) Was William of Orange Protestant or Catholic?
22) How did Parliament limit the power of the monarch in 1689?
23) Who won the Battle of the Boyne in 1690?
24) What did the Irish lose a lot of during the Glorious Revolution?
25) Describe what happened at Glencoe in 1692.
26) Which year was the Act of Union between England and Scotland?
27) Give three reasons why the 1715 rebellion failed.
28) Who led the 1745 Jacobite rising?
29) Who won the Battle of Culloden?
30) In which part of Scotland did people still hate the Hanoverians?

Section Three
Industry, Empire and Reform

Scottish rebellion, led by Bonnie Prince Charlie, fails.	1745	
	1760	George II dies. George III, his son, becomes King aged 22.
Britain gains Canada and the West Indies from the Treaty of Paris with France.	1763	
	1773	Boulton and Watt start making and selling steam engines.
American War of Independence begins.	1775	
The American Continental Congress issue the Declaration of Rights.	1776	
America gains independence from the British after the War of Independence.	1783	
	1789	The French Revolution begins. The monarch, King Louis XVI, is executed in 1793.
	1792	France declares war on Austria. They go to war with most of Europe over the next few years.
	1804	Napoleon crowns himself Emperor of France.
	1805	Napoleon is defeated at the Battle of Trafalgar.
	1807	Slave Trade is banned in the British Empire. Keeping slaves isn't banned until 1833.
The Luddites begin smashing factory machines because they fear will lose their jobs.	1811	
The war with France ends and the Corn Laws are passed.	1815	
	1820	George IV becomes King. He was really greedy and grew very fat.
The Swing Riots take place. The workers protest for more jobs and better wages.	1830	William IV becomes King.
The Reform Bill makes some changes to the voting system and gives more people the vote.	1832	Britain suffers from its first cholera epidemic.
Poor Law Act is passed which says able-bodied poor can only get help in workhouses and the conditions in workhouses should be harsh.	1834	
	1837	Victoria becomes Queen. Famous for wearing black and looking miserable after her husband dies, she ruled for an incredible sixty-four years.
The Chartist group is formed. They campaigned to give more people the vote and drew up the 'People's Charter'.	1838	
Chartist march in London — their petition with 2 million signatures is handed to Parliament.	1848	
Reform Act gives most men the vote.	1867	
The Married Women's Property Act improves the rights of married women.	1870	
Another Reform Act is passed, giving working men in the country the right to vote.	1884	
	1890	Britain colonises Uganda and Rhodesia.
	1901	Edward VII becomes King. He was a rebel, who was fond of women, drink, gambling and travel.
Emmeline Pankhurst founds the Women's Social and Political Union to campaign for women's rights. She is imprisoned several times from 1908-1913.	1903	
	1914	The First World War begins.

The Hanoverians

The Hanoverian period started with the rule of George I in <u>1714</u>, and ended with Queen Victoria's death in <u>1901</u>. The period saw huge <u>political</u>, <u>economic</u> and <u>social changes</u> for Britain.

The *Balance* of *Power Shifted*

1) Since the Glorious Revolution in <u>1688</u> (p. 62-63), Britain had been ruled by a <u>monarch</u> and <u>two houses of Parliament</u> — the House of Lords and the House of Commons.

2) Under the Hanoverians, Parliament <u>increased</u> its <u>political power</u>, and the monarchy <u>handed over</u> a lot of control.

3) This was also the period in which Britain acquired a <u>huge Empire</u> across the world.

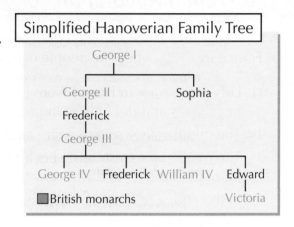

Simplified Hanoverian Family Tree

■ British monarchs

Britain's *Economy Thrived*

At the start of the Hanoverian period, Britain <u>already</u> had productive <u>agricultural</u> and <u>manufacturing</u> industries.

From the 1760s, <u>big changes</u> took place as Britain gradually became the world's <u>first industrial nation</u>.

- <u>Factories</u> were built, using new <u>industrial machinery</u> and <u>techniques</u>.
- <u>Canals</u>, <u>railroads</u>, and the first <u>steam engine</u> allowed goods to be transported faster and over longer distances.
- <u>Extensive trade</u> across the world made huge <u>profits</u> for Britain.

In 1760, Britain imported 1,250 tons of raw cotton, and processed it mostly by hand. By 1840, Britain imported 366 million tons of raw cotton, and processed it mostly in factories.

The *Population Boomed*

1) The <u>population doubled</u> in Britain between <u>1721-1821</u> from 7.1 to 14.2 million.

2) Between 1810-1820, there were 5 or 6 children per family on average, the <u>largest</u> average <u>family size</u> in modern British history.

3) Some of this population growth was because of <u>falling death rates</u>. It was also caused by women <u>marrying younger</u>, and therefore having more time to have children.

4) These <u>social changes</u> were also very closely linked to <u>economic changes</u>. <u>More people</u> meant <u>more workers</u>, which led to <u>more production</u>.

Economic and social change

bigger workforce → thriving economy → better medical care → more children survive to adulthood → population growth → bigger workforce

The whole country didn't change overnight...

All of these changes were important developments in British history, but it didn't all happen at once. Some parts of the country and some groups of people were affected more than others.

The French Revolutionary Wars

Some things didn't change under the Hanoverians — for example, Britain going to war with France. In fact, in the late 1700s, Britain ended up at war with most of Europe.

The French Revolution got rid of the Monarchy

A revolution is a time of sudden dramatic change and new ideas. One of the most famous began in France in 1789, when the people overturned a system that had lasted hundreds of years.

1) Lots of the poor in France were upset with the King, who had introduced huge taxes and did little to improve their poor living conditions.

2) The middle classes were angry about their lack of rights.

3) The nobles were also upset because the King had taken a lot of their power and was now trying to tax them as well.

4) In the end, a revolution took place. There were riots, and rich houses were attacked.

5) The King's prison, the Bastille, was stormed and destroyed in July 1789.

6) In 1793, the King was executed and the French monarchy was abolished. France was declared a republic — a country ruled by the people and their representatives.

Lots of monarchs across Europe were horrified by this. They soon had to deal with the revolutionary forces head on, when France started attacking other European countries.

France went to War with Most of Europe

The French Republic worried that neighbouring countries would interfere and try to restore a monarchy. In order to defend its new system, France ended up going to war with most of Europe, including Britain.

French wars with Europe	
April 1792	France declares war on Austria. Prussia (today's northern Germany and northern Poland) joins with Austria.
Sep 1792	France invades Germany.
Feb 1793	France declares war on Britain and Holland.
March 1793	France declares war on Spain.
June 1794	France takes Belgium.

After some early setbacks, France had a lot of success. From 1795 onwards, they seemed unstoppable, and expanded their territories to control most of Europe.

Britain was the last country still fighting...

Lots of European countries had formed alliances to try and hold back the French forces, but one by one they backed down and made peace treaties. By 1798, only Britain was left fighting.

The Napoleonic Wars

By 1798, only Britain was left in the fight against France. Napoleon, the commander of the French army, had crowned himself Emperor in 1804, and he ruled for the next decade.

*Napoleon made France the most **Powerful** country in **Europe***

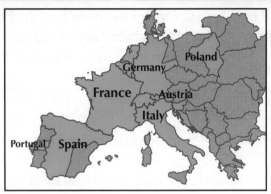

Napoleon's French Empire at its largest (around 1811)

1) Napoleon's great military leadership created a huge French Empire in Europe.

2) At one time, Napoleon's 'Grand Army' consisted of over half a million soldiers from all over Europe. This was roughly ten times the size of most European armies at the time.

3) France controlled part of Spain and Italy, as well as parts of Germany, Austria, Poland, Portugal and other countries.

*The British **Defeated Napoleon** at the **Battle of Trafalgar***

1) Napoleon was desperate to add Britain to his Empire.

2) The British navy was led by Admiral Nelson, a skilled commander who had fought Napoleon several times.

3) By September 1805, Napoleon had a French and Spanish fleet at Cadiz on the southern Spanish coast, in an ideal position to attack the British navy.

4) Nelson and his fleet set out for Cadiz, and met the French near the Cape of Trafalgar, further south. Using risky but intelligent tactics, Nelson destroyed Napoleon's forces, but was shot in the chest and died below deck.

5) The Battle of Trafalgar proved to Napoleon that he could not defeat the British navy. He started thinking of other ways he could attack Britain.

Admiral Horatio Nelson

© Mary Evans Picture Library

*The **Battle of Waterloo** was the **End** for **Napoleon***

1) After an unsuccessful campaign against Russia, and with much of Europe beginning to rise against him, Napoleon gave up his rule in 1814 and was exiled.

2) In 1815, he escaped his guards and travelled back to Europe. When he arrived in Paris, the new king fled to Belgium, and Napoleon took control once more.

3) Napoleon tried to attack the British at Waterloo (a village in Belgium). The British were led by the Duke of Wellington. With help from the Prussians, Napoleon was defeated.

4) He was exiled again, this time by the English, and died a recluse in 1821.

The British Empire

By 1900 the British Empire controlled nearly a <u>quarter of the world</u>. Britain began building its empire in Elizabethan times and it continued to expand until the 1900s through trade, wars and exploration.

The **British Empire** expanded from the 1600s to the 1900s

The Expansion of the Empire

1600 East India Company created. At first it just traded with India, then it started to set up outposts and settlements.

1607 Settlement of Virginia. Network of colonies in the West Indies. Colonised Barbados in 1625.

1700s The British were the biggest slave traders in the world, and benefited from slave colonies, e.g. in Jamaica.

1763 Treaty of Paris — Britain gains huge colonies, e.g. Canada, Senegal, Florida.

1770 Captain Cook claims New South Wales in Australia.

1775 The British lose thirteen American colonies in the War of Independence.

1793-1815 The British gain colonies in wars with France.

1858 Britain takes direct control of India and the East India Company is ended.

1876 Britain receives the rest of Canada through treaties.

1899-1902 British Empire extends over the rest of Australia.

1) During the 1600s and 1700s the <u>expansion</u> of the British Empire was motivated by <u>trade</u>. The idea was to gain as much foreign land as possible because this would be <u>good economically</u> — as a source of <u>raw materials</u> and <u>labour</u> and as a <u>market</u> to export British goods to.

2) During the 1800s Britain continued to gain territory and trading rights. The British Prime Minister Benjamin <u>Disraeli</u> (1804-1881) wanted to expand the Empire. He persuaded the government to buy shares in the <u>Suez Canal</u> which provided a <u>trade route</u> to India and the Far East.

Bombay in c. 1745, when the city was owned by the East India Company. The East India Company shipped silk, tea, cotton, indigo and saltpetre from India and traded them all over the British Empire.

© Mary Evans Picture Library

Written Source

"The entire continent of Africa, the Holy Land, the valley of the Euphrates, the Islands of Cyprus and Canada, the whole of South America, the islands of the Pacific not heretofore possessed by Great Britain, the whole of the Malay Archipelago, the seaboard of China and Japan." *Cecil Rhodes' vision of what the Empire should be. Rhodes was a British colonialist.*

Britain and America

The British first began establishing <u>colonies</u> in America in the 1600s. Sometimes this was done by <u>private trade companies</u>, and other times by <u>religious groups</u> building a new life.

*The **New World** was **Very Attractive** to Britain*

1) Britain hoped that America would provide a <u>trade route</u> to <u>East Asia</u>.

2) There was also a huge variation of <u>resources</u> available, such as tea, cotton and corn. This made America very <u>commercially appealing</u>.

3) In the 1600s, the British began to travel to America and set up <u>colonies</u> — <u>settlements</u> of <u>British people</u> who would bring the local people under their <u>rule</u> and <u>claim</u> the local resources. This process is known as <u>colonisation</u>.

4) The first colony was <u>Virginia</u>. It was founded in <u>1607</u> by a <u>private company</u> hoping to make money from <u>trade</u>.

5) Other colonies were founded by <u>Puritans</u> (very strict Protestants) escaping <u>religious persecution</u> in Europe. For example, <u>Massachusetts</u> was founded in 1620 by Puritans who travelled on a ship called <u>The Mayflower</u>.

6) Once colonisation began, some of the <u>lower classes</u> also travelled to the New World in search of a <u>better life</u>.

The New World is the name Europeans gave to North and South America in this period.

*Britain gained **More Colonies** through **War***

Canada

The Americas

■ British territory from 1763
☐ The original Thirteen Colonies

1) Between <u>1756-1763</u> lots of European powers fought one another to gain control of colonies, including some in the New World. This is called the <u>Seven Years War</u>.

2) <u>Britain did very well</u> out of the war. In <u>1763</u> they signed the <u>Treaty of Paris</u> with France and Spain and Britain <u>gained</u> significant colonies which weren't originally theirs.

3) From <u>France</u>, Britain gained <u>Louisiana</u> east of the Mississippi, all of their <u>territories</u> <u>in Canada</u> and the <u>islands</u> of Tobago, Dominica, St Vincent and the Grenadines. From Spain they gained <u>Florida</u>.

*The **Colonies** were **Quite Free** to start with*

1) By <u>1775</u>, Britain had claimed <u>thirteen</u> colonies in North America.

2) Until the 1760s, the British government largely left the settlements <u>alone</u>. They were too <u>busy</u> with European and Civil Wars.

3) Lots of settlers established democratic <u>town meetings</u>, trial by <u>jury</u>, and operated their own fleets <u>separate</u> from the British navy.

Britain and America

Britain started to **Rule** its colonies more **Strictly**

1) The Seven Years War had cost Britain a lot of <u>money</u>. America was very <u>expensive to protect</u>, and many people in Britain believed that it should <u>contribute</u> more towards its own <u>defence</u>.

2) Britain decided to start <u>taxing</u> the colonies more <u>heavily</u>. The <u>1765 Stamp Act</u> and <u>1767 Townshend Acts</u> were two taxes very unpopular with the American colonists. They <u>protested</u>, sometimes violently.

3) Britain also started to <u>control</u> the <u>imports</u> and <u>exports</u> to and from the colonies more <u>tightly</u>. They said that most American exports could <u>only</u> be sent to <u>British ports</u>, and the colonists could only buy <u>British-made</u> goods.

4) The <u>Tea Act</u> in <u>1773</u> stirred up more <u>protest</u>. It gave the British East India Company (p. 82) a good deal importing tea to America — undercutting other companies. American patriots <u>dumped</u> a shipment of the <u>tea</u> into the <u>sea</u> in protest — this is known as the <u>Boston Tea Party</u>.

Illustration of the Boston Tea Party.

© Mary Evans Picture Library

Thirteen Colonies Rebelled against Britain

1) <u>Patriots</u> in America believed that the new taxes and controls went <u>too far</u>. They felt they were not being treated <u>fairly</u> as <u>British citizens</u>.

2) In <u>1774</u>, representatives from twelve of Britain's <u>Thirteen Colonies</u> formed the <u>First Continental Congress</u>.

3) The Congress <u>wrote</u> to the King, <u>George III</u>, saying:
   - they were <u>loyal</u> to Britain, but Britain had <u>no right</u> to <u>tax</u> and <u>control</u> them in this way.
   - they would <u>stop importing</u> British goods and <u>exporting materials</u> to Britain unless the taxes and controls were <u>removed</u>.

4) George III <u>rejected</u> the petition. Peaceful measures gave way to <u>fighting</u> and the <u>American War of Independence</u> began in <u>1775</u>.

The **Americans Won Independence** in 1783

The War of Independence	
May 1775	Second Continental Congress. They decide they are still loyal to Britain but also form a Continental Army. They write the Olive Branch Petition to George III, asking him to help resolve the differences in a peaceful way. He rejects it straight away.
July 1776	Congress agrees the Declaration of Independence. Until this point, the Continental Army were fighting for their rights as British citizens. Now this changes, and they start fighting for independence. America finds allies in France, Spain and Holland, who are already fighting Britain in Europe, the West Indies and India.
Oct 1781	America and France capture over 7,000 British soldiers in the Siege of Yorktown. After this, Britain agrees to negotiate for peace.
Sept 1783	The Treaty of Paris is signed, recognising the Thirteen Colonies as an independent nation.

Slavery

Britain played an <u>important role</u> in selling millions of Africans into <u>slavery</u> in the New World.

Britain played a Big Role in the Slave Trade

1) The Spanish set up plantations in the <u>West Indies</u> from 1492. They wanted <u>African slaves</u> to work on the <u>plantations</u> there.

2) By the 1600s, the <u>British</u>, <u>Dutch</u> and <u>French</u> had set up <u>trade posts</u> in Africa to <u>sell slaves</u> to the Spanish.

3) Slaves were <u>taken</u> from their families and <u>sold</u> to the European traders. The slaves were <u>crammed</u> onto ships where they were <u>chained</u> in rows, and had to lie in one another's vomit and waste for <u>weeks</u> as they crossed the Atlantic.

4) Slaves were then <u>sold</u> to <u>plantation owners</u> in the West Indies and North America.

5) By the <u>1700s</u> the British <u>dominated</u> the transatlantic slave trade and had <u>plantations of their own</u> in the West Indies and America.

6) The plantations grew crops like <u>cotton</u>, <u>tobacco</u> and <u>sugar</u>, which the plantation owners could sell for big profits back in Britain (see p. 81).

7) At least <u>11 million people died</u> on the way across the Atlantic because of atrocious <u>conditions</u> and <u>treatment</u>. Many millions more became slaves on plantations.

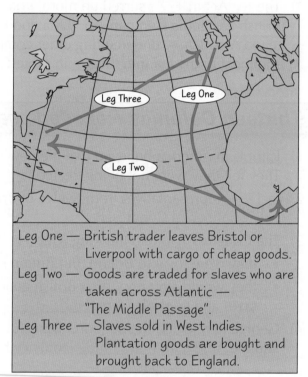

Leg One — British trader leaves Bristol or
                 Liverpool with cargo of cheap goods.
Leg Two — Goods are traded for slaves who are
                 taken across Atlantic —
                 "The Middle Passage".
Leg Three — Slaves sold in West Indies.
                 Plantation goods are bought and
                 brought back to England.

Map showing the 'Triangular Trade' — British trade across the Atlantic.

Conditions on the plantations were <u>incredibly harsh</u>. Slaves had to work extremely <u>long hours</u>, got <u>no pay</u> and were often <u>beaten</u> or even <u>killed</u> by their owners.

Written Source — 1791

"When a ship comes on the coast they send for the traders and make them presents, to encourage them to bring people to sell as slaves. The Black Kings have told me that they go to war to get slaves. I have seen prisoners... delivered to white traders, or else driven down... to the water side for auction to the best bidder." *James Towne reporting to the Committee on the Slave Trade. He is saying that the slave traders often got the different African tribes to capture slaves for them. One tribe would attack another and take prisoners who became slaves.*

Slavery

Slavery was <u>eventually banned</u> in Britain and the USA, but it was a <u>tough fight</u>. People were making a lot of money from slavery and wanted to carry on making a lot of money.

Slavery *Helped* Britain *Economically*

1) Because of the slave trade some <u>ports</u> became <u>busy</u> and <u>rich</u> cities. Bristol, Liverpool, Hull and Lancaster all grew really quickly once the triangular trade started.

2) British people who <u>dealt</u> in the slave trade, either with the <u>slaves</u> themselves or with the <u>products</u>, were some of the <u>richest</u> people in the eighteenth century.

3) The <u>cheap cotton</u> from slave plantations helped to expand Britain's <u>textiles</u> industry, which would form an important part of Britain's <u>Industrial Revolution</u> (p. 86-89).

4) <u>Profits</u> from the slave trade were invested in building <u>banks</u> and funding <u>scientific</u> advances.

People started to *Fight Against* slavery

Slaves lived and died in <u>terrible conditions</u>. People began to demand the <u>abolition</u> of slavery.

1) Some slaves <u>protested</u> by making things <u>difficult</u> for their owners — <u>breaking tools</u> and <u>destroying crops</u> were good ways to disrupt business.

2) Slaves on the plantations sometimes <u>ran away</u>. This was <u>dangerous</u> because they could be severely <u>punished</u> or even <u>killed</u> if they were caught.

3) In Britain, men like <u>William Wilberforce</u> and <u>Granville Sharp</u> fought against slavery in the <u>courts</u> and in <u>Parliament</u>.

4) In the <u>British Empire</u> the <u>slave trade</u> was banned in <u>1807</u>.

5) <u>Keeping slaves</u> was banned in <u>1833</u>. All slaves under 6 were made immediately free, the other slaves had to be 'part slave' and 'part free' for four years — but they had to be paid for any work they did.

William Wilberforce

William Wilberforce was a British politician who campaigned for most of his political life to end slavery. He died just three days after it was banned in Britain.

Olaudah Equiano published a famous book...

Olaudah Equiano was a slave, captured at the age of 11. He worked in Barbados and then on ships, before being brought to work in Europe. He eventually bought his freedom and published his life story. His story helped gain support for the abolition of slavery.

Colonies in India

Britain's interest in India started with trade. In the 1600s companies from England, Portugal and France set up trading posts along the Indian coast. The British increased their power in India and started to colonise parts of it in the 1700s.

The **East India Company** changed from **Trader** to **Ruler**

The East India Company had three main bases in India — Bombay, Madras and Calcutta. These were known as 'The Presidencies', each having a governor in charge of local affairs. These governors had almost total control of their territory, and acted more as government officials than as businessmen.

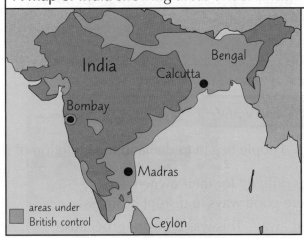

A map of India showing areas under British control in 1805

The East India Company was a British trading company. The Company had its own private armies to occupy territories and defend them against rival traders.

1) Madras was founded in 1639 by the East India Company, and a fort was built there called Fort St. George. Charles II received the Bombay area through marriage and he leased it to the Company in the 1660s. The Company's power rapidly spread from these bases.

2) In 1857-1859 there was a mutiny of the Indian soldiers in the East India Company's army. They were angry because they felt British rule didn't respect Indian culture and traditions. They refused to use new gun cartridges which were rumoured to be greased with cow and pig fat (cows are sacred to Hindus, pigs are unclean to Muslims).

3) They killed some of their officers and the rebellion quickly spread. It was crushed by the British and as a result the Act for the Better Government of India was passed in 1858. The British government took over the governing of India and also took over the Company's army.

India was the "Jewel in the Crown" of the British Empire

1) Economic control of India was a massive advantage to England during the 1800s. Indians had to pay taxes to the British. India was used as a market which British goods could be sold to. Products such as indigo (a dye), tea and cotton were produced cheaply in India for the British market.

2) The Prime Minister Benjamin Disraeli bought shares in the Suez Canal, which opened in 1869 and provided a trade route to India. He persuaded Queen Victoria to be crowned Empress of India in 1876. India was seen as the "Jewel in the Crown" of the British Empire.

The Empire Under Victoria

The **Victorians** were **Proud** of the **Empire**

1) The Victorians were <u>proud</u> of their achievements and the <u>power</u> of the Empire and were keen to <u>celebrate</u> it.

2) <u>Empire Day</u> (Queen Victoria's birthday, May 4th) became a <u>public holiday</u> in Britain in 1902. Children were encouraged to dress up and sing <u>patriotic</u> songs. The last Empire Day to be celebrated was in 1958.

3) Many British people in the 1800s believed the <u>British Empire</u> benefited the colonies because they could have <u>British government</u>, <u>Christianity</u> and <u>education</u>.

4) Many people today would <u>disagree</u> with this attitude — but you've got to remember that <u>at the time</u>, back in the 1800s, colonialism was <u>seen as a good thing</u> by the majority of Britons.

Trading links with the British Empire meant that Britons could buy goods from around the world. This display of fruit, in a Cheshire shop in the early 1900s, includes dates and bananas.

© Chester History and Heritage

A map of the British Empire in 1915

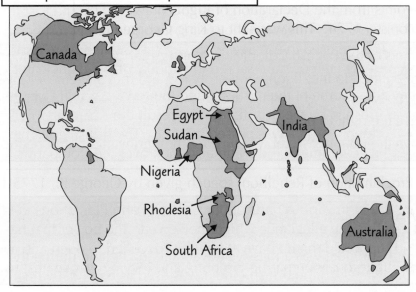

Canada

Egypt

Sudan

Nigeria

Rhodesia

South Africa

India

Australia

The dark side of the Empire...

The British Empire is a pretty controversial topic. Some people today think that the British Empire and other European powers unfairly exploited the resources and people of the colonies.

Sources and Questions

The expansion of the empire had a huge effect on people in England — there were all sorts of new, exotic things available and more countries to trade with.

1 *By 1900, Britain had gained an empire. It is estimated that a quarter of the world's population in 1900 was under British rule.*

Source A — Map showing the British Empire in 1915

Source B — Fruit Shop, early 1900s

Garden Lane Fruit Shop in Cheshire — the display of fruit includes dates and bananas.

a) Study Source A and decide whether these countries were part of the Empire in 1915:
  i) Australia   ii) Canada   iii) The USA   iv) India   v) Brazil

b) Bananas and dates do not grow in cold countries like Britain.
  Use Source A to explain how the shop in Source B was able to stock them.

2 *In the 1760s and 70s Britain started to tighten its control of its American colonies, and taxed the colonists there heavily. Thirteen colonies revolted against British rule, and won independence. Read Sources A and B, and then answer the questions below.*

Source A — Points from the Declaration of Rights drawn up by American colonists, 1774. This was sent to King George III.

The inhabitants of the English Colonies in North America have the following rights:
- They are entitled to life, liberty and property, and they have never given any sovereign power the right to take any of these from them without consent.
- They have the right to participate in legal councils.
- They have the right to assemble, consider their grievances, and petition the king.

Source B — Proclamation of Rebellion, speech given by George III, 1775

Many of our subject in various parts of our Colonies and Plantations in North America...forgetting the allegiance which they owe to the power that has protected and supported them...have at length proceeded to open and avowed rebellion, by...traitorously preparing, ordering and levying war against us.

a) Is this statement true or false?
  "The colonists felt that certain rights had been taken from them by the British."
  Explain your answer using Source A.

b) What do Sources A and B suggest about why the American War of Independence broke out in 1775?

Sources and Questions

3 *Millions of people were taken from West Africa by European slave traders and sold as slaves — mainly in the West Indies and South and North America. Slave ships carried the slaves across the Atlantic in inhumane conditions.*

Source A — Plan of a British slave ship

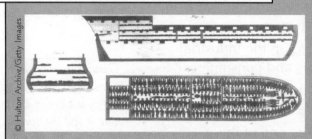

The plan shows how many people the slave traders intended to carry in the lower deck of the ship.

Source B — Extract from Olaudah Equiano's autobiography, 1789

The white people looked and acted, as I thought, in so savage a manner — for I had never seen among my people such instances of brutal cruelty. The closeness of the place, and the heat of the climate, added to the number in the ship, which was so crowded that each had scarcely room to turn himself, almost suffocated us.

a) Is the following statement true or false?
"The plan of a British slave ship in Source A supports Olaudah Equiano's account that conditions on board slave ships were very overcrowded."

b) What information can you learn about the conditions on slave ships from Equiano's account in Source B that you can't learn from Source A?

4 *Individuals like Thomas Clarkson and William Wilberforce played an important role in ending slavery. Read Sources A and B, and then answer the questions below.*

Source A — Rosemary Rees, a modern historian

Thomas Clarkson travelled all over Britain collecting evidence of atrocities committed by slave traders. He interviewed sailors, merchants and black seamen who had once been slaves... He set up local committees for the abolition of the slave trade.

Source B — Description of The Society for the Abolition of the Slave Trade

The Society for the Abolition of the Slave Trade was founded in 1787 by Thomas Clarkson and Granville Sharp. They asked the MP for Hull, William Wilberforce, to support their Society's cause in Parliament. Wilberforce presented a bill to Parliament for the abolishment of the slave trade in 1791, but it was defeated by 163 votes to 88 votes. They continued to campaign and present bills in Parliament. Eventually, in 1807, a bill was passed which made it illegal for a British citizen to transport slaves.

a) Why did Thomas Clarkson interview sailors, merchants and former slaves?

b) Use Source B to explain William Wilberforce's role in helping to end the slave trade.

The Industrial Revolution

The 1700s and 1800s in Britain saw great changes in <u>farming</u>, <u>transport</u> and <u>industry</u>. This is called the Industrial Revolution. Some parts of Britain were more quickly affected than others.

The **Industrial Changes** were **Massive**

1) Between 1800 and 1850 the <u>population</u> of Britain <u>doubled</u> from 9 million to 18 million — the fastest growth ever.

2) The growth in population may have <u>speeded up</u> the Industrial Revolution because it created more <u>workers</u> and <u>consumers</u>.

3) The growth of <u>railways</u> definitely speeded up the Industrial Revolution.

4) The <u>steam engine</u> had been developed at the end of the 1700s by Boulton and Watt. Its use in transport and industry gradually <u>changed</u> Britain's <u>way of life</u>.

5) Over 2000 miles of rail had been laid by 1850, <u>connecting London</u> to most major centres in England.

6) This led to <u>huge growth</u> in industries like <u>iron</u> and <u>coal</u>. Goods could be moved around the country quickly and easily.

Despite technological developments, the average speed of a train in Britain today is still the same as it was in the 1800s.

The Industrial Revolution began slowly. Before the Industrial Revolution many workers, such as weavers, <u>worked</u> at <u>home</u>. Working at home was known as <u>The Domestic System</u>.

New <u>inventions</u> like the Spinning Jenny meant they could increase production to meet demand from elsewhere in the Commonwealth.

At first these new machines were small enough to be kept in homes, but soon they became so big they could only be stored in <u>factories</u> and they needed <u>fewer workers</u> to make them work.

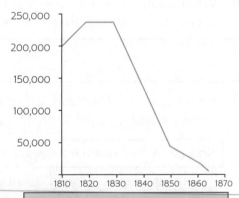

The number of handloom weavers working between 1810 and 1870. This shows that the lives of thousands of people were affected by the introduction of machinery.

Written Source — 1832

"I worked from five in the morning till nine at night. I lived two miles from the mill. We had no clock. If I had been too late at the mill, I would have been quartered. I mean that if I had been a quarter of an hour too late, a half an hour would have been taken off. I only got a penny an hour, and they would have taken a halfpenny." *Elizabeth Bentley, a factory worker interviewed in 1832.*

The Industrial Revolution

The *Rate of Change* was *Different* around the country

Different areas of the country were affected differently by the Industrial Revolution.
The changes didn't take effect everywhere at once — some places still used older methods
and machinery for a while.

1) It took quite a long time for many of the old crafts
to die out. Some people were resistant to the new
machinery and methods — they preferred to use their
old methods and tools.

2) Some changes only affected some parts of the country.
For example, the steam engine in the textile industry
affected workers mainly in the North and Midlands.

3) The changes were applied to some industries more
quickly than others. For example, in 1850 there were
still more sailing ships than steamships because they
were better for long trips.

*The inside of a Lancashire cotton
mill factory around 1830.*

© Mary Evans Picture Library

Some *Cities* got *Bigger*

1) There were new factories and jobs because of
the Industrial Revolution. Industrialised cities
got bigger.

2) Migration had a large part to play in the growth
of the cities. Workers came to the cities from
the British countryside and abroad to find work.
During the Irish potato famine of the 1840s,
nearly a million Irish peasants fled to Britain to
find work and avoid starvation at home.

3) If you look at the map you can see that some
areas of the country have more big towns and
cities than others — some areas were more
industrialised than others.

• Town or city with
population over
100 000

Map of where people lived in 1900

Many factories set up in the North because
they needed to be near coalfields. Coal was
used to power lots of the factory machinery.

Industrial Revolution — not your usual type of revolution...

It might not have been a bloody revolution but the Industrial Revolution is still a pretty
important revolution. Just think, if the steam engine hadn't been invented we could all still be
living in small villages and travelling by horse and carriage.

The Industrial Revolution

New <u>machines</u> and <u>working methods</u> were invented during the Industrial Revolution. This affected the lives of ordinary people dramatically — and not all of them were happy about it.

People were **Afraid** of **Losing Their Jobs**

1) Common land was <u>being enclosed</u> (fenced off). This meant many country people couldn't make a living because they had nowhere to graze their animals.

2) <u>New machinery</u> was being introduced in farming and industry, and many <u>feared for their jobs</u>.

3) <u>Improvements in transport</u> (especially roads and canals) meant industrial changes could happen more quickly.

4) In 1815 thousands of <u>soldiers and sailors</u> came home after the French Wars and found <u>no jobs</u>.

5) The <u>price of wheat</u> was very high, but <u>wages</u> were very low. So people couldn't afford much food. Britain saw the outbreak of <u>several riots</u>.

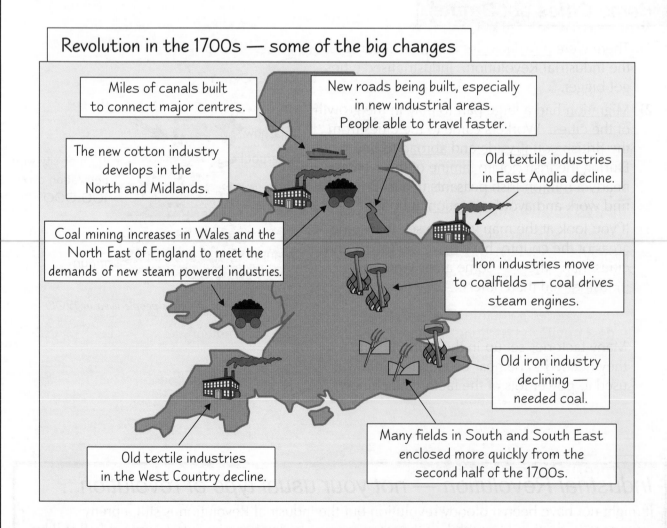

Revolution in the 1700s — some of the big changes

Miles of canals built to connect major centres.

New roads being built, especially in new industrial areas. People able to travel faster.

The new cotton industry develops in the North and Midlands.

Old textile industries in East Anglia decline.

Coal mining increases in Wales and the North East of England to meet the demands of new steam powered industries.

Iron industries move to coalfields — coal drives steam engines.

Old iron industry declining — needed coal.

Old textile industries in the West Country decline.

Many fields in South and South East enclosed more quickly from the second half of the 1700s.

The Industrial Revolution

The Industrial Revolution meant that many jobs were under threat, as people were being replaced by machinery. There were some groups who decided to fight for their jobs.

Different Groups started Riots

1) The Luddites were named after Ned Ludd (a made-up name for their leader — they were too afraid of punishment to use their real names). From 1811 to 1813 they smashed factory machines in the Midlands and the North.

2) The Swing Riots happened in 1830, when farm labourers attacked farmhouses and machinery, demanding better wages and more jobs. They especially hated the new threshing machines that did the work of several men. Their leader was known as Captain Swing.

3) The Rebecca Riots started in the late 1830s — the rioters protested against high tolls (the charges for using the new roads). Their leader wore women's clothes in order to disguise himself.

Luddites attacking machinery in a textile factory.

Some people say that the leader in the Rebecca Riots had been given clothes by a lady called Rebecca.

Others say that it refers to a passage about Rebecca in the Bible.

Rioters were Executed or Deported

1) The Government came down harshly on all the people involved in these riots.

2) They executed many of them, or transported them to Australia as convicts.

3) A law of 1812 carried the death penalty for those breaking machinery.

4) Poor people who lost their jobs often had no way to survive other than by turning to crime.

The Government acted like this because:

- they worried something like the French Revolution might happen here (less privileged sections of society overthrowing the government).

- they thought the poor had no right to say what should happen.

- many of them were landowners who wanted these changes to happen.

Written Source — 1812

"I was asked by my men to give you warning to pull down your detestable shearing frames. If you do not, I shall detach 300 men to destroy them... and we will burn down your building to ashes... murder you and burn all your housing." *A letter from Ned Ludd to a factory owner.*

City Slums

The Industrial Revolution made <u>Britain</u> incredibly <u>wealthy</u> and <u>powerful</u>, but many of the <u>people</u> who worked in these new industries lived in <u>poverty</u> in areas called <u>slums</u>.

The *Industrial Revolution* created *Slums*

1) The Industrial Revolution brought more and more people into the <u>towns</u> and <u>cities</u>. Housing had to be built very <u>quickly</u>.

2) The houses were <u>packed tightly in rows</u> and were of a <u>poor quality</u>. Areas of housing like this were called <u>slums</u>.

3) The houses were <u>damp</u>, with <u>no running water</u> or proper <u>sewage</u> system. Four or five families often lived in <u>one house</u> and shared an <u>outside toilet</u> with even more neighbours.

4) The slums were built <u>near</u> to the factories so that workers could travel there easily. This meant that the slums were badly <u>polluted</u>, <u>noisy</u> and <u>unclean</u>.

5) Sewage was stored in <u>cesspits</u>, <u>rivers</u> or even the <u>street</u>. The cesspits sometimes overflowed.

© Rischgitz/Getty Images

A London slum, polluted by train smoke.

In 1858 hot weather caused the Thames water level to drop, leaving all the waste behind. The smell was so bad that it became known as the Great Stink.

The people in the *Slums* were *Very Poor*

1) The people in the slums worked <u>long hours</u> for <u>low wages</u>.

2) Many people couldn't afford <u>doctors</u> or <u>medicine</u>, or enough <u>food</u> to feed their family.

3) There was no <u>unemployment benefit</u> or <u>pensions</u> for the elderly. <u>Workhouses</u> were the <u>only help</u> available for the poor. They provided basic <u>food</u> and <u>shelter</u> in exchange for working <u>long hours</u> in <u>brutal</u> (and often <u>dangerous</u>) conditions.

4) Most people couldn't afford to send their children to <u>school</u>. Instead, children as young as <u>five</u> were sent out to work for up to <u>sixteen hours</u> a day.

© Mary Evans / Iberfoto

An illustration from Dickens' Oliver Twist, showing children in a Victorian workhouse. Lots of orphaned children had to go to the workhouse when their parents died.

Written Source — 1889

"Since 1861 the population of Lewisham has increased fourfold, and building is still in rapid progress... Some of the new building, perhaps much of it, is, however, shoddy — not long for this life, and some of it is likely to deteriorate rapidly." *From 'Life and Labour of the People', a report published by Charles Booth, which showed that 30% of Londoners lived in poverty.*

Cholera

With cramped and damp living conditions, no clean running water and sewage flowing into the street, disease was rife in the Victorian slums. Cholera is a particularly nasty example.

Cholera *is a* Horrible Disease

1) Cholera is an infectious disease. It arrived in Britain from the East in 1831. Just one year later, it had become an epidemic.

2) Cholera spreads when infected sewage gets into drinking water. It causes extreme diarrhoea and patients often die from dehydration.

3) Both rich and poor people caught the disease, but it was particularly widespread in the slums. Here there was no proper sewage system and people were packed together in crowded living conditions, so germs could spread quickly from person to person.

4) There were more epidemics in 1848, 1853-4 and 1866.

> *Epidemic: a disease that is widespread in a community at a certain time.*

Preventing cholera became a Priority

The Government tackled cholera by improving water supplies and building a sewer system. Two men had really important roles in these improvements.

John Snow

1) John Snow linked cholera to contaminated water.

2) He studied an outbreak in an area of London in 1853-4, and realised that all the victims were drinking from the same water pump.

3) He removed the handle from the pump, and the outbreak ended. The Government realised that they needed to improve the water and sewage systems urgently.

Joseph Bazalgette

1) Joseph Bazalgette was the chief engineer appointed to build a massive sewer system for London.

2) The sewers collected the waste and took it away from heavily populated areas. About 1300 miles of sewers were constructed.

3) Bazalgette's system helped to prevent cholera. It was officially opened in 1865, and has since been copied by most cities in Western Europe.

Joseph Bazalgette
© Illustrated London News Ltd/Mary Evans

The cholera epidemics highlight an important problem...

Cholera demonstrates that the slums in Britain's cities and towns were very bad for people's health. With no clean water and or sewage system, disease was widespread. Gradually, the Government started to work with local councils to provide more help for the working classes.

Middle Class Victorians

The Victorians believed in a class system. The upper classes were rich enough not to have to work. The working class had the worst, badly paid jobs. And the middle class was growing all the time...

The **Middle Class Grew** during the 1800s

The middle class grew during the 1800s. This was due to a number of factors —

1) The Industrial Revolution and the growth of the British Empire had a positive effect on Britain's economy. In the 1800s it was a wealthy nation, which could sustain a middle class of professionals, bankers, shopkeepers and merchants.

2) The Industrial Revolution meant that cities were growing and new cities were being established. The British population was also increasing rapidly. People worked in a greater range of jobs with a greater range of incomes.

3) The growth of the railways, banking system and civil service led to an increase in middle class professionals running the administration. There was also a growth in other professions such as law and medicine.

There was an increase in **Civic Pride**

1) Cities were growing fast during the 1800s. In 1700 20% of the population lived in cities — by 1850 it was 55%. At first some of these cities weren't very nice places to live — they had grown too fast to have many public services.

2) There was an increase in civic pride in the late 1800s — people felt proud of the towns and cities they lived in. Wealthier Victorians spent money on the foundation of public parks, libraries, swimming baths and town halls.

3) There were also major Victorian building projects like the new Houses of Parliament in 1872 and the beginning of the London underground railway in 1863.

It was very much the done thing for wealthy Victorians to spend time in public parks like Hyde Park. Appearances were really important for Victorians, so strolling in parks was a way of showing off new clothes or accessories.

Hyde Park in 1885.

© Illustrated London News Ltd/Mary Evans

New cities were an eyesore...

By the mid 1850s the new towns and cities were the place to be seen. However, many wealthy Victorians were used to living on beautiful country estates so the industrial cities would have looked really ugly to them. That's why some of them funded things like building parks to make the towns and cities look more attractive.

Middle Class Victorians

The Victorian middle classes had **New Leisure Activities**

1) With the <u>railways</u> came the possibility of day or weekend trips to the <u>seaside</u>. Resorts such as <u>Brighton</u> became popular.

2) <u>Spa towns</u> such as Bath and Buxton also grew in popularity. Victorians would go there to "take the water" for their health.

3) The Victorians enjoyed the <u>theatre</u> and <u>music hall</u> very much. Music hall was a bit like a variety show of singers, comedians and other performers.

4) The Victorian middle classes also loved <u>sport</u>. Many national games were developed at this time, for example <u>rugby</u> and <u>cricket</u>. The great cricketing hero of the day was W. G. Grace.

The orderly Victorians left their mark on sports. It was the Victorians who were responsible for making official rules and regulations for sports. Before the Victorians wrote the rules for football it had been a much more violent game — sometimes men had been so badly injured they were unable to work again.

Victorian Sporting Timeline

1823	The first game of Rugby was alleged to have taken place at Rugby School.
1863	Football Association (FA) formed.
1866	The Amateur Athletic Club formed.
1871	Rugby Football Union founded.
1877	The first official cricket test match.

Many of the middle class had **Strict Moral Values**

1) The Victorian middle classes praised the values of <u>thrift</u> (saving), <u>self-reliance</u> and personal <u>achievement</u>.

2) Many were attracted to groups such as the Methodists who preached <u>against</u> drinking <u>alcohol</u> and <u>gambling</u>. This is probably why the Victorians have a reputation for being prim and proper, and a bit strict.

Written Source — 1890

"For women... beauty of face and form is one of the chief essentials, but unlimited indulgence in violent outdoor sports, cricket, bicycling... and — most odious of all games for women — hockey, cannot but have an unwomanly effect on a young girl's mind." *Badminton Magazine.*
Victorians thought that only some sports were suitable for women, like tennis and skating.

Sources and Questions

There are loads of sources from Victorian times, which makes it easier for historians to work out what life was like then. These questions will get you to practise finding information from sources.

1   *The introduction of machines during the Industrial Revolution meant that workers who had previously produced goods by hand might lose their livelihood. Sources A and B are evidence of their opposition.*

Source A — From a letter sent to a Huddersfield factory owner in 1812, signed 'Ned Ludd'

Sir,

We have been informed that you own some of these detestable shearing frames... I warn you that if they are not taken down by the end of next week, I shall send one of my lieutenants with at least 300 men to destroy them... and if you have the impudence to fire at any of my men, they have orders to murder you and burn all your housing. Have the goodness to go to your neighbours and inform them that the same fate awaits them if their frames are not taken down...

Signed by the General of the Army of Redressers

Ned Ludd

shearing frames = machines which could make cloth

redressers = people who seek justice

Source B — J. F. Aylett, a modern historian

The government used harsh measures to stop the violence. In 1812, machine-breaking became a capital crime. Anyone found guilty was hanged. One 16 year old was hanged just for acting as sentry, while his brothers destroyed a factory.

a) Answer the following questions about Source A.
   i)   Why was the letter written to the factory owner?
   ii) What were the Luddites (supporters of 'Ned Ludd' and the anti-machinery movement) threatening to do?
   iii) Is the threat from one man or a group of men? Explain your answer.
   iv) Why do you think the letter is signed 'Ned Ludd' rather than with the author's real name?

b) What evidence is there in Source B to back up the claim that the government used 'harsh measures to stop the violence'?

Sources and Questions

2 *The Industrial Revolution changed Britain dramatically but different areas changed at different speeds and in different ways. Look at the two maps below and answer the questions that follow.*

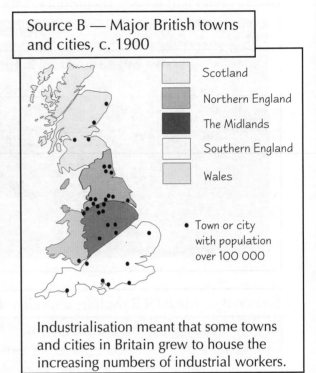

Source A — Main canal systems in Britain, c. 1900	Source B — Major British towns and cities, c. 1900

Scotland
Northern England
The Midlands
Southern England
Wales

canal

Canals were used to transport goods from one place to another. Areas which were heavily industrialised usually had a canal network.

Scotland
Northern England
The Midlands
Southern England
Wales

• Town or city with population over 100 000

Industrialisation meant that some towns and cities in Britain grew to house the increasing numbers of industrial workers.

a) Use Source A to decide whether the following areas were probably heavily industrialised, partly industrialised or not industrialised:
   i) Scotland
   ii) Wales
   iii) Southern England
   iv) Northern England
   v) The Midlands

b) Use Source B to decide whether the following areas were probably heavily industrialised, partly industrialised or not industrialised:
   i) Scotland
   ii) Wales
   iii) Southern England
   iv) Northern England
   v) The Midlands

c) Looking at your answers to questions a) and b), write a paragraph about which parts of Britain were industrialised and which were not. Give reasons to back up your answer.

Sources and Questions

3 *In Victorian England many middle class and upper class people were well-off and could afford good housing. Working class people often lived in really awful conditions.*

Source A — Railway arches and housing in Victorian times

© Rischgitz/Getty Images

Source B — Michael Rawcliffe, a modern historian

In the rapidly growing towns and cities, those who could afford to often moved out into the suburbs. Here the new homes were not so densely packed together. Semi-detached villas were popular with the middle classes. A large Victorian house was built for one family and its servants.

Source C — A description of back-to-back housing in Leeds, 1842

In one street in Leeds there are 34 houses, and usually there are about 340 people living in these houses — that's ten in every house. The aim of the property developers seems to have been to build as many cottages as possible in the smallest possible space. This is how whole neighbourhoods end up without a water supply or toilets.

a) Sources B and C both describe houses in Victorian England. Which one describes houses similar to those in Source A? Give one reason for your choice.

b) What evidence is there in Source A that many people lived in housing which was:
   i) overcrowded?
   ii) unhygienic?
   iii) in a polluted environment?

c) What evidence is there in Source C that many people lived in housing which was:
   i) overcrowded?
   ii) unhygienic?

d) The middle classes often lived in better housing than the working classes.
   Using Sources B and C, find one example of a way in which middle class housing (Source B) was preferable to working class housing (Source C).

SECTION THREE — INDUSTRY, EMPIRE AND REFORM, BRITAIN 1745-1914

Sources and Questions

4 *Victorian Britons loved to spend time by the seaside in towns like Brighton. Study Sources A, B and C and answer the questions below.*

Source A — A description of the work of Dr Richard Russell in the 1700s

Dr Richard Russell's writings convinced other doctors and their patients that drinking and bathing in (Brighton) sea-water would help treat many conditions, especially diseases of the glands... The coastal resort of Brighton was one of the nearest beaches to London (just 6 hours by stagecoach) where they could get the sea-water treatment that Dr Russell recommended.

Source B — Facilities introduced at Brighton 1823–1900

1823	Royal suspension chain pier built, so that boats could moor in the town
1849	Brighton Pavilion (George IV's palace) bought by the town
1864	Grand Hotel built
1866	The West pier opened
1872	Aquarium opened
1874	A museum, park and library opened
1883	Opening of Volk's electric railway along the sea front — the first electric public transport
1888	A clock tower built for Queen Victoria's golden anniversary
1900	The Palace pier (Brighton pier) opened

Source C — A rhyme from the 1800s

I took the train to Brighton — I walked beside the sea,
And thirty thousand Londoners were there along with me.

a) Source C shows that Brighton was very popular with visitors in the 19th century. What reason for the popularity of Brighton is suggested in Source A?

b) In Source B find 5 things that Victorians visiting Brighton could do.

c) According to Source C what was the downside of visiting Brighton?

d) Imagine you live in Victorian London and have taken the train to Brighton for a day by the seaside. Write a postcard home in which you describe your day. Use Sources A, B and C to help you.

Voting Reform

The political situation in 1830 was elitist and corrupt — less than 2% of the population had the right to vote. Eligibility to vote depended on property, gender and where you lived. Open voting (everyone knew what you had voted) meant voters were sometimes pressured or bribed.

The **1832 Reform Bill** made **Changes** to the **Voting System**

The 1832 Reform Bill brought in measures to improve the voting system —

1) 56 Rotten Boroughs were abolished.

2) More parliamentary seats were given to growing industrial cities.

3) It extended voting rights for men.

4) This meant 300,000 extra voters — now about 3% of the population had the right to vote.

5) The working class gained little — but these early changes meant that further reform would probably be easier in the future.

> Rotten Boroughs — these were small constituencies, with very few voters, which could nevertheless send two MPs to parliament (because they'd always been able to). For example, Old Sarum near Salisbury was an old fort — no one lived there, but it still had two MPs. There were 56 such boroughs in 1831.

There were **Two** major **Political Parties** at the time

Britain had two main political parties during the nineteenth century — the Whigs and the Tories.

The Whigs

1) They believed that the people and their representatives had the power, so the ruler should serve their wishes.

2) Whigs were associated with the 'new' wealthy class, such as merchants and bankers, and with more reforming ideas.

3) It was a Whig Prime Minister, Charles Grey, who saw through the Reform Act in 1832 (though he had to get the King to create 100 new Lords to get it passed).

Portrait of Charles Grey.

© Mary Evans Picture Library

The Tories

1) In simple terms, the Tories believed that the ruler held the power, and that the people should serve their wishes.

2) They were associated with the 'old' class of landowners and traditional politics.

3) In 1834, Sir Robert Peel became Prime Minister, and took the Tories in a new direction towards controlled reform. This approach was more like the Conservative Party of today.

The Reform Act changes weren't dramatic...

The 1832 Reform Act didn't change anything for most people. Most men still didn't have the vote and many people were scared they would lose their jobs — so they turned to trade unions, which provided help and support for workers when they needed it.

Voting Reform

The Chartist Movement wanted more Reform

The Chartist movement was basically a working class movement, formed in the 1830s. They felt Parliament didn't care about working class issues, and worked out a 'People's Charter' for more reforms. It contained six points they wanted to be made law —

Events that led to the Chartist group forming	
1815	End of wars with France. Corn laws passed which kept bread prices high.
1819	Peterloo massacre — 13 people killed when cavalry charged a meeting in St Peter's fields in Manchester.
1831	Riots after the Reform Bill failed to gain House of Lords approval.
1832	Parliamentary Reform Bill.
1838	Chartist group formed.

1) A vote for every adult male over 21 — so poorer people could vote.

2) A secret ballot — voters would be protected from pressure from candidates.

3) Annual parliaments.

4) No property qualifications for MPs — so poorer people could become politicians.

5) Payment of salary for MPs — so you didn't have to be rich to become one.

6) Constituencies with equal numbers of voters — so a large city would have more MPs than a small town because it would have more constituencies.

Support for the Chartists Grew when there was high Unemployment

The Chartist movement gained support at first because —

1) People were angry that so little had been done for the working class by the 1832 Reform Act.

2) Working people were angry about the 1834 Poor Law Act which brought in workhouses.

3) The 1830s and 1840s were a period of economic depression with widespread unemployment.

4) The middle class saw Chartism as a way to gain further reform of parliament.

The Chartists presented three petitions to parliament in 1839, 1842 and 1848. There were also some violent protests, e.g. the 1839 Newport riots and the 1842 Stoke riots.

The Chartist movement Failed

The Chartist movement eventually failed because —

1) The leadership of the movement was divided on whether to use violent or peaceful methods.

2) In the 1850s and 1860s the economic situation was improving — so people were less angry about their situation.

3) Over time, most of the Chartists' demands became a part of British law anyway.

Written Source — 1848

"Many signatures are in the same handwriting. We also see the names of distinguished people, among them her Majesty as Victoria Rex. Other names to be seen are the Duke of Wellington and Sir Robert Peel. Many names are obviously fictitious such as 'No Cheese', 'Pug Nose'..."
Spokesman in the House of Commons on 14 April 1848 making fun of the Chartist's petition.

Voting Reform

Lots of tricky terms in these few pages. 'Franchise' and 'suffrage' both mean the right to vote — especially the right to vote in political elections. It took a while for women to get it...

There was another Reform Act in 1867

Despite the failure of the Chartist movement, their demands were campaigned for again, from 1865, by the Reform League. With rapid economic and social change many people felt that parliament still didn't fairly represent the people. Benjamin Disraeli's government passed the Reform Act of 1867, which meant:

1) The vote was given to all male householders living in urban areas.

2) Most ordinary working men in the towns got the vote if they were over 21 and were householders or lodgers paying more than £10 a year rent.

3) The number of voters increased to about two million men.

There were now a few boroughs, like Oldham, where most of the voters were working class.

Punch was a popular Victorian magazine that often mocked Victorian politics and politicians.

This picture is about the Reform Act — the horse has Disraeli's head and it is jumping into the unknown. This is what many people at the time thought about the Reform Act, that giving so many working men the vote was a big unknown and that it could all go horribly wrong. Disraeli was Prime Minister at the time of the 1867 Reform Act.

PUNCH, OR THE LONDON CHARIVARI—August 3, 1867.

REFORM

A LEAP IN THE DARK.

© Mary Evans Picture Library

Cartoon from Punch magazine, published 3 August 1867.

The Reform Act in 1884 made even more changes

1) This Act extended the vote to working men in the countryside.

2) For the first time all of the United Kingdom was under the same electoral system.

3) Local government became more democratic. Elected town and county councils replaced many functions of magistrates and Poor Law Unions.

Written Source — 1865

"The Tories are afraid of 5 million men who are shut out by the present system of representation, but who could vote if they went to live in the Cape, Australia or Canada."
John Bright, Liberal MP, arguing for parliamentary reform in 1865.

Voting Reform

The *Status* of *Women* was changing

In some ways the status of women improved during the 1850-1900 period —

1) Custody of children improved after the Caroline Norton case. After separating from her violent husband, Caroline was banned from seeing her children. She wrote pamphlets protesting against the existing laws. Her arguments helped get the Marriage and Divorce Act of 1857 passed, which gave women more rights when it came to marriage and their children.

2) There were wider employment opportunities. Nursing was now a respectable occupation, following the example of Florence Nightingale. Increasing numbers of women were gaining employment in clerical work, shop work and the professions.

3) The Married Women's Property Acts of 1870 and 1882 improved married women's rights.

4) The Co-operative Women's Guild (1884) campaigned for women worker's rights, divorce reform and better schools and pensions.

5) By 1901 some women were allowed to vote in local elections.

Women Weren't really Protected by the Law

In other ways women's position in society was still really bad in the 1850-1900 period —

1) Women's legal status was still limited.

2) Women's employment was still mainly low paid, and conditions for factory work were poor. Women who didn't have the support of a husband or family were exploited.

3) Contraception was limited and primitive. Many women spent much of their adult life pregnant and giving birth — which was dangerous to their health.

4) Women's reform groups were seen as a threat. Many articles were written against the 'New Women' and Women's Suffrage (voting rights).

By *1900* there were still Inequalities

1) There was widespread support for a limited measure of Women's Suffrage.

2) The electoral system was still a long way off from a modern idea of 'democratic'.

3) Other political and social issues were often regarded as more important than Women's Suffrage.

4) The Liberal Party was the most likely to bring in Women's Suffrage. But some Liberals thought if rich women got the vote they would vote Conservative — so they weren't so keen.

Victorian Britain was a man's world...

Being a woman in Victorian times wasn't much fun. They couldn't vote and had very few legal rights. Even Queen Victoria didn't want women to have the vote.

Women's Rights

Victorians had clear roles for both men and women and they didn't like it when people didn't behave like they were supposed to...

Many **Victorians** thought **Women** should stay at **Home**

1) Women didn't get the <u>right to vote</u> in national elections in Britain until <u>1918-1928</u>.

2) In Victorian times women had far <u>fewer rights</u> than men. For example, until 1882 married woman couldn't own property — everything they owned became their husband's property on marriage.

3) Most Victorians believed men and women should have very <u>different roles</u> in <u>society</u>.

<u>Men</u> could take responsibility and be involved in the <u>public sphere</u> of life —
- Business and finance
- Politics and government
- The law and trade

<u>Women</u> were viewed as the '<u>Angels of the house</u>', who took responsibility for the <u>private sphere</u> —
- Care of children
- Managing the household
- Cooking, washing, cleaning

© Hulton Archive/Getty Images

Victorian governesses and nursemaids in 1880.

Whether women **Worked** depended on **Class**

1) <u>Poorer women</u> worked because their families needed the <u>extra income</u>. They had jobs in mills, mines, domestic service or at home. They were <u>paid less</u> than men.

2) <u>Middle class women</u>, though, would aim to <u>marry</u> well and not have to work. Instead they would learn <u>female accomplishments</u> such as singing, playing the piano, sewing and managing the household. As the "angel of the house" they were supposed to be dutiful and obedient.

Education wasn't supposed to be for women either...

The first university college for women wasn't opened until 1869. Many scholars believed that women had smaller brains than men and that they were too emotional to be able to study at higher levels.

Women's Rights

Learn about these **Three Campaigners** for **Women's Rights**

Different groups campaigning for women's rights had different ways of drawing attention to their cause and different leaders.

Josephine Butler 1828-1906

1) Josephine Butler came from a <u>rich family</u> but became increasingly angry about the way women (especially <u>poor, underprivileged women</u>) were treated by Victorian <u>society</u>.

2) In 1864, 1866 and 1869 the <u>Contagious Diseases Acts</u> were passed. Parliament was worried about the spread of <u>sexually-transmitted diseases</u> in the navy and armed forces. The Acts allowed policemen to <u>force</u> any woman they suspected of being a prostitute to have a <u>medical examination</u>. Josephine Butler thought this was <u>degrading</u> and sexist. She <u>campaigned</u> for 21 years until the Acts were repealed.

3) Her campaigning methods included touring the country making <u>speeches</u>, and <u>writing</u> letters and pamphlets.

Harriet Taylor 1807-1858

1) She wrote a series of <u>essays and articles</u> which set out clear ideas on improving the status of women and their rights. She did a lot of work with her second husband John Stuart Mill, but it wasn't credited to her.

2) She <u>suggested new laws</u> to protect women from violent husbands (1851).

3) A key book, '<u>The Subjugation of Women</u>' was completed after her death by her husband JS Mill and her daughter Helen. Her daughter later became active in the Women's Suffrage campaign and the Kensington Society (which produced the first petition requesting votes for Women).

Emmeline Pankhurst 1858-1928

1) She helped form the <u>Women's Franchise League</u> in 1889, which pressed for women's rights.

2) In 1903 she founded the <u>Women's Social and Political Union</u> (WSPU) to gain more publicity for women's rights — its motto was "Deeds not Words".

3) Between 1908-13 she was imprisoned several times for <u>civil disobedience</u> (demonstrating, breaking up political meetings, stone throwing) and went on hunger strikes while in prison.

4) WSPU action was suspended on outbreak of war and its efforts turned to a patriotic support and recruitment of women to help the war effort.

© Time Life Pictures/Getty Images

Emmeline Pankhurst being arrested.

Written Source — 1912

"This is our policy, short of taking human life we shall stop at no step we consider necessary to take... Our militant policy is fixed and unalterable." *Speech made by Emmeline Pankhurst, saying that almost nothing would stop the suffragettes fighting for their cause.*

Women and the Vote

Fighting for women's right to vote wasn't easy — it took years of protesting and a world war to make things change, but eventually it happened.

Many Victorians **Argued Against** giving **Women** the **Vote**

<u>Arguments against</u> allowing women more rights included —

1) A belief that women's work and responsibilities were in the <u>home</u>.

2) <u>Medical opinion</u> on the differences between men and women, e.g. men had bigger brains than women and were therefore cleverer, or that women were 'hormonally unstable'.

3) A belief that women were the <u>weaker sex</u> and needed to be protected.

4) A belief that women were more <u>individualistic</u> and would be unable to co-operate, e.g. in politics.

5) A belief that women would allow their <u>emotions</u> to affect their decisions about law and politics.

Some **Famous Victorians** supported women's suffrage

1) <u>John Stuart Mill</u> was one of many <u>influential writers</u> arguing for improvements in women's rights and status. He was the husband of Harriet Taylor (see p. 103).

© London Stereoscopic Company/Getty Images

© Hulton Archive/Getty Images

2) <u>David Lloyd George</u> was the <u>leader</u> of the <u>Liberal Party</u>. He had some sympathy for women's suffrage but was strongly against the violent methods of the WSPU. He was <u>elected Prime Minister</u> in <u>1918</u> in the first general election in which some women were allowed to vote.

Written Source — 1913

"Now that it is pretty well assured women will vote, it is time to arouse public sentiments in favour of Votes for Babies. The awful state of our Government shouts aloud for the infant suffrage... Let the babies vote! For that matter let the cows vote." *From the Gentleman's Journal in May 1913. Its view is typical of some men at the time who thought it was a silly idea to let women have the vote.*

Women and the Vote

Campaigners used Different Tactics to gain publicity

Suffragists

Suffragists used <u>peaceful</u> and constitutional means to campaign for women's suffrage. They —

1) wrote letters
2) <u>wrote articles</u> and journals
3) produced <u>petitions</u>
4) held <u>public meetings</u>
5) tried to gain the support of MPs.

Suffragettes

Suffragettes lost patience with peaceful tactics and used more <u>provocative methods</u>. They —

1) heckled and broke up political meetings
2) <u>smashed windows</u> by stone throwing
3) made <u>personal attacks</u> on MPs and their homes
4) went on <u>hunger strike</u> when imprisoned
5) <u>sought publicity</u> — for example by chaining themselves to railings.

The First World War sped up the pace of change

Things changed for women during the <u>First World War</u> (1914-1918). They —

1) Took on many <u>traditional male jobs</u> — drivers, engineers, etc.
2) Worked in the <u>Women's Land Army</u> — replacing farmworkers who had gone to fight.
3) Worked to produce weapons in <u>munitions factories</u>.
4) Were able to take on <u>more responsibility</u> and to <u>act independently</u> of men.

Suffrage Timeline

1910 onwards	A majority of MPs supported Women's Suffrage. Many also wanted universal voting for men.
1914-1918	First World War — women took on traditionally male jobs.
1918	Vote given to all men over 21 and women over 30 who are householders or the wives of householders.
1928	Women given the vote on equal terms to men.

The Suffragettes — from prison to citizenship...

Some suffragettes put themselves in danger for their cause. At the 1913 Derby, Emily Davison ran out in front of the King's horse carrying a suffragette banner — she was trampled to death.

Sources and Questions

From 1850-1890 several changes were made to extend the franchise — people who could vote.

1 *The second Reform Act was passed in the summer of 1867. Benjamin Disraeli was the Prime Minister. Robert Lowe was an MP against the Reform Act being passed.*

Source A — Prime Minister Disraeli on why he favours reform, March 1867

Looking to what has occurred since the Reform Act of 1832 was passed — to the increase of population, the progress of industry, the spread of knowledge, and our ingenuity in the arts — we are of the opinion that numbers, thoughts and feelings have since that time been created which it is desirable should be admitted within the circle of the Constitution.

Source B — Cartoon, 1867, showing Prime Minister Disraeli as a horse

© Mary Evans Picture Library

Source C — Robert Lowe, speaking against reform, May 1867

Now, what do you know of the non-electors of this country? What are their politics? What are their views? What will be their influence for good or evil upon our institutions? Two years ago... I said that if we embarked on the course of democracy we should either ruin our party or our country. Sir, I was wrong, as prophets very often are. It is not a question of alternatives; we are going to ruin both.

a) Using Source A, decide which of these statements is most accurate.
  i) "Disraeli felt that a larger number of people deserved the vote because they had skills and ideas which they should be allowed to voice."
  ii) "Disraeli felt that a larger number of people deserved the vote because the 1832 Reform Act was awful didn't recognise the arts or the progress of industry."

b) Which speech, Source A or Source C, most closely matches the view shown in Source B?

c) Do you think it was only politicians who opposed the 1867 Reform Act? Explain your answer using Source B.

d) Using Sources B and C, why were some people afraid of widening the franchise?
  i) They thought enough people had the vote already.
  ii) They thought the working classes were like horses.
  iii) They didn't know what would happen as a result.

Sources and Questions

There were lots of different groups fighting for women to get the vote, and there are lots of sources about it. Here are a few to help you answer the following questions.

---

2 *The suffragette movement campaigned for women's right to vote.*

Source A — A suffragette poster published during the First World War

a) Read the list of words below and answer the questions about Source A:

> immoral   criminal   well-educated   responsible   worthwhile   irresponsible

   i) Choose three words from the list that describe some of the women in the poster.
   ii) Choose three words from the list that describe some of the men in the poster.

b) Which of the statements below best describes the message of Source A?
   i) Women can't vote. Even if a woman is a mayor or a doctor she can't vote.
      Men can vote. Even if they have been drunkards or criminals men can vote.
   ii) Only women who have good jobs, e.g. doctors, can vote.
      All men can vote unless they are lunatics, drunkards, etc.

3

Source A — L. E. Snellgrove, a modern historian

As the debates and votes in Parliament produced no results, on 16 February 1912, Mrs. Pankhurst said she intended to bring into action "the time-honoured, official argument of the stone." Then, on 1 March 1912, the owners of some of London's most expensive shops found out that she had not been joking.

Source B — Lucy Burns, a suffragette in Holloway Prison

We remained quite still when ordered to undress. The Governor blew his whistle and a great crowd of wardresses reappeared, falling upon us forcing us apart and dragging us towards the cells. I fell helplessly to the floor. One of the wardresses grasped me by my hair and literally dragged me along the ground.

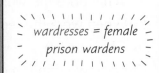

wardresses = female prison wardens

a) Use Source A to suggest the kinds of action that suffragettes like Mrs Pankhurst took to get their cause noticed.

b) Lucy Burns was sent to prison as a punishment for her activities as a suffragette. According to Source B, how was she treated in prison by the wardresses?

Summary Questions

From the French Revolution to American Independence, and the Luddite riots to the Chartist Movement, this was certainly a period of big political and social changes for Britain and the rest of the world. Have a go at these summary questions to make sure you've taken it all on board.

1) "Economic and social changes during the Hanoverian period were very closely linked." True or false?

2) In which country did a revolution begin in 1789?

3) Who became Emperor of France in 1804?

4) Who commanded the British navy at the Battle of Trafalgar?

5) a) What was the name of the major private trading company created in 1600?
   b) Give two examples of goods that this company transported.

6) What is meant by the word 'colonisation'?

7) a) When was the Treaty of Paris signed?
   b) Which two countries signed this treaty?
   c) Who gained territories in the New World as a result?

8) Give two examples of acts introduced for British New World colonies in the 1760s and 1770s.

9) How many colonies rebelled in the American War of Independence?

10) a) Which continent did most slaves come from during the Transatlantic Slave Trade?
    b) Who dominated this trade in the 1700s?

11) Give two ways in which the Slave Trade helped Britain economically.

12) When were these things banned in the British Empire?
    a) the slave trade
    b) keeping slaves

13) Which country was known as the 'Jewel in the Crown' of the British Empire?

14) "The Victorians were very proud of their Empire." True or false?

15) "The whole of Britain was transformed instantly by the Industrial Revolution." True or false?

16) Which group smashed factory machinery between 1811 and 1813?

17) Why did the Government crush industrial rioters so harshly? Give at least two reasons.

18) Give two ways in which working class housing in towns and cities was of poor quality.

19) Why did cholera spread so quickly in the Victorian slums?

20) Write a short paragraph to explain why the middle class grew during the 1800s.

21) Describe three types of leisure activity enjoyed by the Victorian middle classes.

22) Write a paragraph explaining two differences between the Tories and the Whigs in the mid-nineteenth century.

23) Who were the Chartists?

24) What does the word 'franchise' mean?

25) When were the second and third Reform Acts?

26) Give two ways in which the position of women in society was bad in the 1850-1900 period.

27) Give two things men were considered responsible for and two things women were considered responsible for in Victorian society.

28) Why did many Victorians believe women shouldn't vote? Give at least three reasons.

29) Write a paragraph explaining the differences between suffragists and suffragettes.

30) In what year were women given the vote on equal terms to men?

Section Four
Britain and the Wider World

The National Insurance Act passes, providing sick pay and unemployment benefit for many workers. — **1911**

1914 — Archduke Franz Ferdinand is assassinated. International alliances in place at the time means that this escalates into World War One.

1916 — The Battle of the Somme leaves over a million soldiers dead or wounded.

1918 — The Armstice begins at the eleventh hour of the eleventh day of the eleventh month, bring World War One to an end.

1919 — Germany signs the Treaty of Versailles, losing land and accepting blame for the outbreak of the war.

Ireland is split into two.
Southern Ireland becomes independent. — **1920**

1922 — Egypt is officially granted independence, but Britain continues to have a lot of power in the country.

The Wall Street Crash in the USA causes a global depression. — **1929**

1933 — Hitler becomes Chancellor of Germany and quickly establishes a dictatorship.

1938 — Germany and Austria unite — this is called Anschluss. Kristallnacht — the Nazis attack Jewish businesses and synagogues.

1939 — Germany invades Poland. Britain declares war on Germany and millions of children are evacuated from London.

Churchill becomes Prime Minister and rationing is introduced in Britain. The First Blitz takes place from September 1940 to May 1941. — **1940** — Germany invades France.

The Beveridge Report recommends cradle to grave welfare. — **1942** — Hitler begins his Final Solution at Auschwitz-Birkenau.

The Second Blitz sees heavy bombing in Britain from June 1944 to March 1945. — **1944**

Allied troops close in on Berlin.

1945 — Hitler commits suicide on April 30.

India wins independence, but is split into India and Pakistan. — **1947** — The atomic bomb is dropped in Hiroshima and Nagasaki in August, leading to Japan's surrender and the end of World War Two.

The National Health Service is founded in Britain. — **1948**

The *Empire Windrush* arrives in the UK, bringing over 400 immigrants from the Caribbean.

1956 — The Suez crisis reaches its peak when Britain and France invade Egypt.

The Notting Hill Race Riots break out in London. — **1958**

1967 — BBC Radio 1 is launched to broadcast pop music to a young audience.

A group of women protest at the Miss World competition at the Royal Albert Hall. — **1970**

1974 — A fuel shortage leads to the introduction of the three day working week.

The Sex Discrimination Act passes, making it illegal to discriminate on the grounds of sex or marital status. — **1975**

1978 — The 'winter of discontent' sees strikes and power cuts throughout the country.

Margaret Thatcher becomes Britain's first female Prime Minister. — **1979**

1989 — The World Wide Web is launched.

1995 — 16 million people worldwide have access to the Internet.

2000 — 300 million people worldwide have access to the Internet.

2013 — Nearly 4000 million people worldwide have access to the Internet.

World War One

World War I (1914-1918) was known as 'The Great War'. It was 'Great' in terms of the huge numbers of casualties and the involvement of countries across the world.

The world in the early 1900s was Dominated by European Powers

From the early 18th century European countries were building Empires. Having an overseas Empire was a show of power and many conflicts began due to the 'scramble for colonies' — particularly in Africa. In Europe, there was fierce rivalry between the European nations.

1) The British Empire was the largest empire held by a European country. It included Canada, India and Australia.

2) The newly-formed (in 1871) Germany had ambitions to be as big and powerful as Britain.

3) The two countries competed to have the largest navy and army, and the biggest Empire.

Europe Divided into powerful Alliances

To try and balance the power in Europe, the major countries allied themselves into two groups. The idea was that they would be so powerful that they could never fight each other — and Europe would have to stay at peace. Unfortunately, there was a lot of tension between the two sides. An arms race began, with each country competing to have the biggest army and navy in Europe.

The Triple Alliance (also called the Central Powers):

In 1882 Germany, Austria and Italy formed an alliance. They promised to help each other should they go to war. The Ottoman Empire joined in 1914. Italy switched sides in 1915.

The Triple Entente:

By 1907 France, Russia and Britain had formed an alliance. They also promised to help each other should they go to war. In 1917 Russia withdrew from the Entente and the war, but the USA joined at about the same time.

Germany saw the Triple Entente as a Threat

1) In 1905 German generals drew up the Schlieffen Plan — a strategy to defeat an attack by the Entente countries if war broke out. The plan involved quickly defeating France, before attacking Russia. The generals thought Russia would take too long to get ready for war, and France was weak, so both would be easily pushed aside.

2) War became almost inevitable by the early 20th century. Many people (and governments) actually wanted a war at the time — but a reason was needed for one to begin.

The Triple Alliance and Triple Entente are easy to confuse...

And it's only going to get worse unless you learn them now. It's pretty simple when you get the hang of it — but vital if you want to know which side a source might be talking about.

World War One

The *Assassination* of *Archduke Ferdinand* started the move to *War*

The <u>shooting</u> of <u>Archduke Ferdinand</u> sparked the First World War.

The lead up to War in 1914	
28 June	The heir to the Austrian Throne, Archduke Franz Ferdinand, was shot whilst visiting Sarajevo by a Serbian nationalist.
28 July	Austria threatened to declare war on Serbia unless it met certain demands. Serbia couldn't meet them, so Austria attacked.
29 July	Russia had promised to protect Serbia, and began to prepare for war.
1 Aug	Britain mobilised the Navy ready for war. Germany declared war on Russia.
3 Aug	Germany declared war on France.
4 Aug	Germany invaded neutral Belgium. Britain declared war on Germany.
6 Aug	Austria declared war on Russia.
12 Aug	Britain and France declared war on Austria.

Franz Ferdinand

© Mary Evans Picture Library/WEIMAR ARCHIVE

Most of the *War* was *Fought* in the *Trenches*

The war began with <u>cavalry charges</u> and open battles. Both sides soon realised that these tactics were <u>useless</u> against modern weapons. Soldiers had to dig trenches to protect themselves.

1) Trench warfare resulted in huge casualties — in the <u>Battle of the Somme</u> in 1916 over a <u>million soldiers</u> were killed or wounded.

2) <u>Conditions</u> in the trenches were <u>terrible</u>. Men were living and fighting in cold, muddy and rat-infested huts cut into the mud. <u>Trench foot</u> and other diseases were <u>very common</u>.

3) It took <u>four years</u> for the Triple Entente to eventually gain an advantage over the Central Powers. A blockade of the German ports by the Royal Navy meant that Germany was <u>out of food, oil</u> and <u>metal</u> to build guns. The fighting ended in <u>November 1918</u>.

A young soldier in the trenches.

© Roger Viollet/Getty Images

4) Millions of soldiers and civilians died in the First World War. To remember these people, as well as all the civilians and soldiers who have been killed in every other war, we hold a two minute silence every year — on <u>November 11th</u> at <u>11.00 AM</u>. This was the moment in 1918 when the <u>armistice</u> (cease-fire) was signed and the fighting of the First World War ended.

Written Source — World War One

"As far as the eye could see was a mass of black mud with shell holes filled with water. Here and there broken duckboards, partly submerged in the quagmire — here and there a horse's carcass sticking out of the water — here and there a corpse. The only sign of life was a rat or two swimming about to find food and a patch of ground." *Private H. Jeary, Queen's Royal West Surrey Regiment, describing no man's land.*

World War One

After the War, most of the major European nations were bankrupt and millions were dead.

Germany was Blamed for the war

Although the fighting had ended in <u>November 1918</u>, the war hadn't <u>officially ended</u> — Germany had to sign a <u>treaty</u> to end the war. But the treaty itself caused <u>problems</u>.

> In 1919 a peace treaty was drawn up by...
> * <u>David Lloyd George</u> — The British Prime Minister.
> * <u>Woodrow Wilson</u> — The US President.
> * <u>Georges Clemenceau</u> — The French Prime Minister.

No-one from the defeated countries of Germany or Austria was invited to the discussions. The paper became known as '<u>The Treaty of Versailles</u>' after the French palace where the leaders met. It was decided that:

1) Germany was to blame for starting the war.
   This was known as a '<u>war guilt</u>' clause.

2) Germany was asked to pay £6600 million in <u>reparations</u> to pay for damages done to France and Belgium (where the fighting on the Western front had taken place).

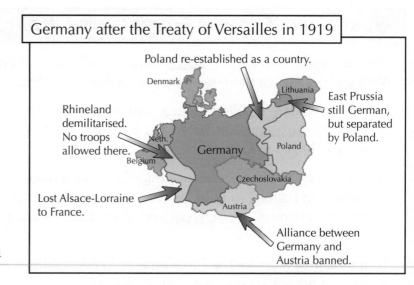

Germany after the Treaty of Versailles in 1919

Poland re-established as a country.

Denmark

Rhineland demilitarised. No troops allowed there.

Neth.

Belgium

Germany

Lithuania

East Prussia still German, but separated by Poland.

Poland

Czechoslovakia

Lost Alsace-Lorraine to France.

Austria

Alliance between Germany and Austria banned.

3) Germany <u>lost land</u> in Poland, France and Czechoslovakia.

4) All of Germany's <u>colonies</u> (e.g. in Africa) were given to the Entente countries.

5) The Austrian Empire was <u>broken up</u> and Austria was forbidden to <u>ally</u> with Germany.

6) A <u>League of Nations</u> was set up. The idea behind it was that countries would meet to discuss problems and find peaceful solutions. The League had <u>no army</u> and not all countries were members (for example the powerful USA <u>never joined</u>).

7) Germany had to <u>limit</u> her army to 100,000 men, the navy to 6 battleships and was banned from building planes or tanks. All German troops had to be withdrawn from the <u>Rhineland</u>, Germany's main mining and industrial area.

Written Source — 1919

"The Allied governments affirm, and Germany accepts, the responsibility of Germany and her allies for causing all the loss and damage to which the Allied governments and their peoples have been subjected as a result of the war." *Treaty of Versailles — the 'War Guilt' clause.*

World War One

Germany was Unhappy with the Treaty of Versailles

Germany had good reason to be annoyed with the Treaty of Versailles —

1) The huge reparations meant that Germany was almost bankrupt — Germany was already suffering from the enormous cost of the war itself.

2) Germany felt vulnerable to foreign attack because her army and navy were so small.

3) Germany felt that it was unfair for its side to take full blame for the war.

4) Germany felt unfairly punished by the loss of its colonies and some of the mainland. Germany felt it had been weakened and split apart.

5) They felt that the treaty was a 'Dictat' (an order) and were upset not to have been invited to Versailles.

6) Many Germans felt that since Germany hadn't actually been invaded, and controlled more land at the end of the war than it had done at the start, that they hadn't really lost the war. Many Germans thought that their government had betrayed them.

The League of Nations was never really Effective

1) The League of Nations did have a number of successes — for example it managed to prevent war between Yugoslavia and Albania in 1921.

2) However the League also had a number of failures — it didn't intervene to stop the Italian dictator Mussolini invading Abyssinia in 1935, other than to try and block exports to Italy, which didn't work.

3) In the following years, Hitler rearmed Germany, occupied the Sudetenland and allied with Austria — which were all clearly going against Versailles. The League did very little to stop him.

4) By the start of World War Two it was clear that the League had failed in its main objective of preventing another war.

5) The League of Nations was abandoned in 1945 and remodelled to form the United Nations (an organisation of countries with peace-keeping aims). Unlike the League, the UN gives more power to certain countries and does not require 100% support from its members to be able to take action. It is more powerful and successful as a result.

In a league of their own...

The political leaders didn't really consider the consequences when they started the First World War. They thought that it would be over by Christmas 1914, but it took four years and millions of lives to end the war — a tragic waste of life.

Sources and Questions

The First World War was horrendously violent — more than 20,000,000 soldiers died and even more were wounded.   You'll need to look carefully at the sources to answer the questions.

1 *By the early 1900s, some European countries had joined together to protect themselves against each other. There were two big groups — the Triple Alliance and the Triple Entente.*

Source A — The Triple Alliance of 1882, with (from left to right) Germany, Italy, and Austria

© History Wiz

Source B — A modern account of the tension in Europe

The Triple Alliance (Germany, Italy, and Austria) and the Triple Entente (Britain, France, and Russia) grew suspicious of each other. When the heir to the Austrian throne was murdered, it led to a war that could have happened at any time, for many different reasons.

a) Using Source A, which countries joined in the Triple Alliance?

b) Why do you think Italy is shown standing on tiptoe in Source A?

c) Read Source B. What was the incident that sparked the outbreak of the War?

2 *The First World War helped develop new and terrible weapons. Look at the sources and answer the questions which follow.*

Source A — Part of a poem by a First World War soldier, Wilfred Owen

GAS! Gas! Quick, boys! An ecstasy of fumbling,
Fitting the clumsy helmets, just in time —
But someone still was yelling out and stumbling
And floundering like a man in fire or lime…
Dim, through the misty panes and thick green light
As under a green sea, I saw him drowning.
In all my dreams, before my helpless sight,
He plunges at me, guttering, choking, drowning.

Source B — Victims of gas attacks

© Three Lions/Getty Images

a) What do you think Source A means by 'As under a green sea, I saw him drowning'?

b) Using Sources A and B, give two of the most frightening things about the use of gas in warfare.

Sources and Questions

3 *The First World War ended with the Treaty of Versailles.*
Look at the sources and answer the questions which follow.

Source A — Conditions for Germany in the Treaty of Versailles

1) Germany was to pay £6.6 billion for the damage caused to France and Belgium by the war.
2) It was not allowed an army of more than 100,000 men.
3) It was only allowed 6 battleships in its navy.
4) It was not allowed to have an air force.
5) Part of its land was given to other countries.

Source B — Poverty in post-war Germany. Women search for food in a rubbish dump.

© Three Lions/Getty Images

a) Name three punishments from Source A that were imposed on Germany.

b) Using both Sources A and B, suggest why the first point in Source A was so serious.

4 *The Treaty of Versailles set up the League of Nations, to make sure there would be world peace in the future. Look at Sources A to C and answer the following questions.*

Source A — A 1919 cartoon about the League of Nations. The title of the cartoon is 'Overweighted'.

© UniversalImagesGroup/Getty Images

OVERWEIGHTED.

Source B — A quote by Mussolini, the Italian leader 1922-1943

"The League is very well when sparrows shout, but no good at all when eagles fall out."

Source C — A modern account of the League of Nations

The League of Nations hoped to bring peace to the world. Yet when nations like Japan, Italy, and Germany challenged it the League did nothing — but it did settle conflicts in places like Greece.

a) What do Source A and Source B say about what people thought of the League of Nations?

b) Read Source C. Which three nations caused the League of Nations problems?

c) Does Source C suggest that the League of Nations was a complete failure?
   Explain your answer.

The Great Depression

The Great Depression was triggered by the Wall Street Crash in the USA in 1929.

The **American Stock Market Crashed** in **1929**

1) In the 1920s, the USA was the <u>richest</u> country in the world.

2) During the '<u>Booming Twenties</u>', the USA loaned billions of dollars to help European countries <u>recover</u> from the effects of the First World War.

3) Wages were high and many Americans could afford to buy new <u>mass-produced goods</u> like radios and refrigerators.

4) American companies were <u>selling</u> lots of goods, so people <u>borrowed</u> money to <u>buy shares</u> in them.

> When you buy a 'share', you buy a part of a business.

5) However, by the end of the 1920s American businesses were <u>producing</u> more goods than they were <u>selling</u>. This meant they were no longer <u>making as much money</u> as before.

6) In <u>1929</u>, the American <u>stock market crashed</u>. People realised some companies were no longer doing so well, and rushed to <u>sell their shares</u>. Shares quickly fell in value and a lot of people and businesses lost money.

7) The stock market in the USA is based on <u>Wall Street</u>, and this crash became known as the <u>Wall Street Crash</u>.

8) Businesses <u>collapsed</u> and thousands of people were <u>ruined</u>. This was the start of the <u>Great Depression</u> which affected many other countries across the world.

The **Depression Affected** other **Industrial Countries**

1) In 1929 the USA <u>stopped lending</u> money abroad. It also asked for <u>repayments</u> from countries it had loaned money to.

2) Most industrial countries were affected — banks failed, industries struggled, and trade ground to a halt.

3) Within three years there were over <u>2.5 million</u> people unemployed in Britain, and more than 30 million unemployed in the industrial countries of the West.

4) <u>Germany</u>, which had relied on American loans after World War One, was particularly <u>badly affected</u>.

© Keystone/Getty Images

Huge crowds of people gathered opposite the stock market on Wall Street as the price of shares began to crash.

The Wall Street Crash — a depressing subject...

The Wall Street Crash had a massive effect on economies across the globe. The world didn't fully recover from the effects of the Wall Street Crash until after World War Two.

The Depression in Britain

The Wall Street Crash had a serious effect on the economy in Britain.

Unemployment Varied across Britain

1) In the 1930s Britain was affected by an economic depression. The economy struggled and there was very high unemployment.

2) Old industries, such as coal, steel and shipbuilding, were the worst affected. There was a fall in demand for these goods. Also, these industries relied on old, outdated machinery and couldn't compete with other countries.

3) These industries were mostly based in Scotland, Wales and the north of England, so unemployment in these areas was high.

4) Newer, 'light' industries producing cars and consumer goods (such as vacuum cleaners and toasters) were growing. These were mostly based in the south of England, so unemployment in this area was not as high.

The Government had to tackle the Problem

1) High unemployment meant that fewer people were paying taxes and more people were claiming benefits. This meant that the government was spending more money than it was getting in.

2) The government wanted to balance the budget. This meant not spending more money than they were getting in taxes.

3) By the end of 1931, the government introduced measures that it hoped would boost the economy and raise money to fund benefits.

New Taxes

1) A 10% tax was placed on goods bought in from outside the British Empire in order to encourage British industry.

2) Income tax was increased to cover increased government spending.

Spending Cuts

1) The government made spending cuts in order to afford the increasing amount paid in unemployment benefits. The wages of public sector employees, such as the police and armed forces, were cut by 10%.

2) Unemployment benefits were cut by 10% and a means test was introduced (see p. 118).

3) These measures saved money so that the government could continue to pay unemployment benefits, but they made life harder for many.

Depression in 1930s Britain — a North-South divide...

Unemployment in 1930s Britain varied a lot from county to county. In 1934, unemployment in Glamorgan, Wales, was more than four times as high as in Surrey, in South East England.

The Depression in Britain

Unemployed people who paid National Insurance (see p. 143) could claim unemployment benefit for 26 weeks. After this, they had to apply for a second benefit called the dole.

Life on the Dole was Tough

1) When they had work, men could usually earn a decent living wage. However, dole payments for a <u>family of four</u> were only about <u>half as much</u> as the average wage.

2) Many families didn't have enough to eat. Eggs and meat were a <u>rare luxury</u>. The basic diet for many was <u>bread, jam and tea</u>.

3) Many people became <u>physically unfit</u> because of their bad diet. Few people died of starvation, but <u>malnutrition</u> was widespread.

4) Many children suffered from <u>diseases</u> such as bronchitis, tuberculosis and rickets. <u>Death rates</u>, particularly for children, were <u>higher</u> in areas affected by the depression.

5) Families could rarely afford <u>new clothes</u>. Many children went barefoot all year.

The Means Test made thing Worse

From 1931, the government created a new way of deciding how much money people could claim on the dole. This was called <u>the means test</u>. It helped the government <u>save money</u>, but it was <u>very unpopular</u>.

1) Inspectors were sent to families who had applied for the dole to see <u>how much money</u> they had. The amount of money a family received was based on the results of the means test.

2) The dole was <u>cut</u> if anyone in the family was <u>working</u> or had a <u>pension</u>. This included any children or grandparents living at home.

3) Many families were told to spend any <u>savings</u> or sell their <u>possessions</u> to pay for food, before they were entitled to the dole.

Some People Protested in Support of the Unemployed

1) Throughout the 1930s, the National Unemployed Workers Movement (<u>NUWM</u>) encouraged strikes and hunger marches to London. They wanted the government to do more to help the unemployed.

2) However, the government <u>ignored</u> the NUWM. It argued that change should be made through the <u>parliament</u> — not through protests which sometimes ended in <u>violence</u>.

The unemployed were poor and powerless...

Life for the unemployed in Britain during the depression was tough, but unfortunately there was very little they could do to make the government change its policies.

Sources and Questions

1   *The Wall Street Crash in the USA in 1929 led to a global economic crisis.*

Source A — A modern description of The Wall Street Crash

The worst day in stock market history took place on the 29th October 1929. A record 16 million shares were sold at a loss. The day became known as 'Black Tuesday'.

Source B — Newspaper headline, October 1929

© Icon Communications/Getty Images

a) Which of the following statements do you think is true?

   i)   The Wall Street Crash saved people a lot of money.

   ii) The Wall Street Crash was a very exciting time.

   iii) The Wall Street Crash caused widespread alarm.

b) How do Sources A and B support your answer?

2   *In the 1930s, Britain suffered from an economic depression and high unemployment.*

Source A — A hunger march, c.1935

© Keystone/Getty Images

Source B — Diners at a show in London, 1938

© Kurt Hutton/Getty Images

Source C — A speech given by the leader of a hunger march

It was my duty to see that the hunger marchers in 1932 marched against the national government of starvation, war and degradation, and paved the way for the smashing of the means test... Comrades, we did not come here for fun. We came for business and we are not going back until the dirty means test as every unemployed man knows it, is taken away from the statute book.

a) Look at Source A. Why do you think unemployed workers, like those in this picture, called their protest 'a march against starvation'?

b) Look at Sources A and B. Do you think that the depression in the UK in the 1930s affected everyone equally? Give reasons for your answer.

c) Look at Source C. How did unemployed workers feel about the means test? Why did they feel this way?

The Rise of Hitler

Within 20 years of the Treaty of Versailles (see p. 112), Europe was at war again. Millions more civilians would die in the Second World War, as well as countless millions of soldiers.

The effects of Versailles were still being felt in the 1920s

The Treaty of Versailles destroyed the German economy in the 1920s. Many Germans had lost their savings and their jobs. Money was worthless — people had to carry wheelbarrows containing billions of Marks just to buy a loaf of bread. Germany needed someone who could solve their problems — and Adolf Hitler made them believe he was the man for the job.

Hitler promised:

1) To reduce unemployment and end the economic crisis.

2) To reverse the Treaty of Versailles and rebuild Germany.

3) To get rid of the people he felt were destroying Germany, e.g. the Jews, the Gypsies, the communists and others.

Money being burnt for heat because it was worth less than firewood in 1920s Germany.

Hitler rose to Power in the 1930s

The life of Adolf Hitler	
20 April 1889	Born in Austria.
1914	Serves in World War One.
1919	Joins the German Workers Party.
1920	Becomes leader of the party and renames it the National Socialist German Workers' Party (Nazis).
1921	Sets up the SA (Stormtroopers) to intimidate people.
1923	Tries to seize power in the Munich Beer Hall Putsch. Fails and is sent to prison.
1924	In prison, writes "Mein Kampf" ("My Struggle") in which he outlines all his views, e.g. hatred of Jews. Plans to take power through democratic elections.
1924	Nazis win 32 seats in the Reichstag.
1929	The Wall Street Crash in the USA. The Great Depression affects Germany.
1932	Nazis win 230 seats in Reichstag elections becoming the single biggest party.
1933	Hitler becomes Chancellor and within a few months establishes himself as a dictator.
1935-39	Hitler goes against the Treaty of Versailles and builds up the German military which enables him to unite with Austria and invade Poland.
1939-1945	World War II and atrocities of the Holocaust.
1945	Commits suicide in his Berlin bunker after marrying his girlfriend Eva Braun.

Reichstag = the German parliament

Hitler promised Germany the world...

The German people were desperate for help after the First World War. They wanted a leader who could provide them with jobs, food and a feeling of pride. Hitler offered them the chance to rebuild Germany — he had popular appeal, strange as it may seem today.

The Rise of Hitler

There's **Debate** about whether **Hitler** was a **Democratic Leader**

Once Hitler became Chancellor he quickly gave himself <u>unlimited power</u>, and ruled without the Reichstag — he became a dictator. Historians still argue about whether Hitler rose to power <u>democratically</u>. These are the main arguments for each side...

Arguments that Hitler came to power democratically:

1) The Nazi party won seats <u>democratically</u> in elections.

2) The Nazi party became the <u>biggest party</u> in the Reichstag due partly to the German voting system, which meant that small parties could easily gain seats and become more <u>powerful</u>.

3) Hitler passed the <u>Enabling Act in 1933</u> democratically which meant he could <u>legally</u> make decisions <u>without</u> the support of the parliament.

Arguments that Hitler came to power undemocratically:

1) The Nazis used <u>intimidation</u> and the threat of the <u>SA</u> (Hitler's private army) to scare voters.

2) The Nazis <u>banned</u> opposition meetings and <u>beat up</u> opposition politicians.

3) The Nazis arrested people who opposed them — after a fire destroyed the Reichstag the Nazis blamed and arrested the <u>communists</u>, even though it was probably the <u>Nazis</u> who started the fire.

4) The Nazis controlled the newspapers and radio. This meant that <u>opposition</u> to the Nazis <u>couldn't get attention</u> in the media.

Hitler with Italian dictator Mussolini in 1938. The crowds are cheering them.

Hitler **Expanded** Germany's **Territory** and **Military**

1) Hitler was determined to make Germany great. In order to do so he wanted to create 'Lebensraum' (living room) for Germans. Many Germans <u>supported</u> this idea.

2) Hitler promised (and delivered) jobs, economic stability, and pride in Germany. People were <u>desperate</u>, and so many supported Hitler <u>despite</u> his hatred of the Jews.

3) Many people in Germany and abroad didn't think Hitler was doing <u>anything wrong</u> by overthrowing the Treaty of Versailles — it was thought the treaty was <u>unfair</u> and Germany had been punished enough. So people did <u>nothing</u> when Hitler began to rebuild the army, build tanks and planes and expand German territory.

4) Britain at this time was following a policy of <u>appeasement</u> — which meant using peaceful <u>negotiation</u> rather than force to deal with any problems.

Written Source — 1938

"My good friends this is the second time in our history that there has come back from Germany to Downing Street peace with honour. I believe it is peace in our time."
Chamberlain, the British Prime Minister, after signing an agreement giving Germany part of Czechoslovakia — an example of British appeasement.

World War Two

Hitler grew more *Confident*, but the *Allies* still did *Nothing*

In the late 1930s, Hitler's policies became more aggressive. Britain and France hoped that they could solve the issue diplomatically — they didn't want another war.

Hitler's aggressive action	Allied response to Hitler
1) Rearmament — Hitler began to rearm after becoming Chancellor. In 1935 he announced that he was expanding the Navy and Air Force. By 1936 the army had hundreds of thousands of soldiers, far more than the Versailles treaty said Germany could have.	1) Britain and France built up their own armed forces but didn't do anything to stop Hitler from building up Germany's — even though Versailles banned it. In 1935 Britain signed the Anglo-German Naval Agreement, which made it legal for Germany to expand its fleet.
2) In 1936, German troops marched into the Rhineland — a demilitarised zone (no soldiers were allowed there) in Germany, near the French-German border. It contained most of Germany's coal and factories.	2) The British didn't think that Germany was doing anything wrong marching soldiers into its own land. France wanted to do something about Germany — but Britain wouldn't help, so France didn't do anything.
3) In 1936, Hitler made alliances with Italy and Japan.	3) The Allies couldn't do anything to stop Hitler because he wasn't doing anything wrong by making alliances.
4) In 1938 Hitler united Austria and Germany (called Anschluss) — which was illegal under the Versailles treaty. He claimed it was a peaceful union, but Germany had threatened Austria and bullied the Austrian chancellor into resigning two months before Anschluss took place.	4) The Austrians asked the Allies for help to keep the country safe until they could hold a vote to ask the Austrian people if they wanted to be a part of Germany. The Allies did nothing to help.
5) In 1938, Hitler invaded the Sudetenland (a German-speaking part of Czechoslovakia).	5) Hoping to prevent war, Britain and France decided to let Germany have the Sudetenland on the condition that Hitler did not invade the rest of Czechoslovakia.
6) In March 1939 Hitler invaded the rest of Czechoslovakia.	6) Did nothing but agreed that if Hitler invaded Poland then they would react.

The Allies hoped they could avoid war...

Britain and France hoped they could control Hitler. They were wrong. Every time they didn't react, Hitler got more confident in his plans to expand German territory.

World War Two

In *September 1939* Hitler invaded *Poland* and *World War 2 Began*

On September 1st, 1939, German troops marched into Poland. The Allies decided that they had to act, and so declared war on Germany.

The Allies
• Britain (and the Empire and Commonwealth)
• France
• USSR (from June 1941)
• USA (from December 1941)

The Triple Axis
• Germany
• Japan
• Italy

© Hulton Archive/Getty Images

The front page of the 'Evening Standard' newspaper after Britain declared war.

1) Initially, the USSR made a pact with Germany and invaded Poland alongside the Germans in 1939. Russia joined the Allies when it was invaded by Germany in 1941 in Operation Barbarossa.

2) There wasn't much fighting in the first few months of the war. Germany didn't invade France until May 1940.

3) The Americans didn't join the war until the Japanese bombed the US fleet at Pearl Harbour (in Hawaii) in 1941, almost destroying it.

The *Second World War* really was *Global*

The Second World War really did involve the whole world. Almost every country was involved in some way with the war. There were several main areas of fighting, or 'theatres'.

1) The Western theatre — This included France, Britain, Germany and the Netherlands. The D-Day landings and Battle of Britain happened in the Western theatre.

2) The Eastern theatre — This included Poland, Russia, the Balkans and Eastern Europe. There was intense fighting here when Germany invaded Russia in 1941.

3) The Pacific theatre — This included Japan, China, and the USA. Many British territories, such as Burma, Singapore and Hong Kong, were also involved.

4) The North African theatre — Here German and Italian forces fought Britain, France and America for control of Egypt (with the Suez Canal).

5) The Mediterranean theatre — This included Italy, Malta and Greece. Italy surrendered to the Allies in September 1943.

6) The Atlantic theatre — German U-boats (submarines) tried to stop supplies reaching Britain by sea.

The war finally ended in 1945. Germany surrendered in May and Japan followed in August. Italy had surrendered in September 1943. Mussolini, the Italian leader, was killed on April 28th 1945 by Italian rebels. Hitler committed suicide in Berlin two days later. The dropping of the atom bombs on Hiroshima and Nagasaki in August 1945 forced Japan to surrender.

The Home Front

Even before war was declared, the government was <u>planning</u> for the worst.

Children were **Evacuated** as a **Precaution**

1) The government worried that the Germans would <u>bomb</u> British cities and that many people would die. They encouraged parents to send their children to the <u>countryside</u> to protect them.

2) Evacuation began on 1 September 1939. <u>Millions</u> of children, as well as <u>pregnant women</u> and mothers with babies, were evacuated. School children travelled with their <u>teachers</u>.

3) However, because the cities weren't bombed immediately, many children <u>returned home</u> for Christmas. A second evacuation had to take place when the <u>Blitz</u> began in mid-1940.

Evacuation was different for everyone

1) Children had very <u>different experiences</u> of evacuation. Many were very happy with their host families. They learnt new things and made new friends.

2) Others had very bad experiences. Some were even made to <u>work</u> for their host families.

3) For many children it was <u>difficult to adjust</u> to country life. Most had no idea when they would be returning home and many were homesick.

4) Carers also had <u>problems</u> with evacuees. Most had <u>very few clothes</u>, some had fleas and most were completely unused to the <u>lifestyle</u> and <u>food</u> of the countryside.

Rationing was introduced in **1940**

1) The government introduced <u>rationing</u> to make sure that no-one went <u>short of food</u> during the war.

2) Food including meat, butter, milk eggs and sugar were rationed, as were clothes and furniture.

3) <u>Spare land</u> (such as local parks and playing fields) was dug up to <u>grow more food</u>.

> *People sometimes traded goods illegally. This was known as the 'black market'.*

Churchill became a **Famous Wartime Leader**

1) Churchill had been both a soldier and a government minister during World War One, so he was very experienced.

2) During the 1930s Churchill had <u>opposed appeasement</u> (peaceful negotiation, see p. 121). He didn't trust Hitler, and wanted Britain to prepare to fight Germany.

3) When Churchill became Prime Minister in 1940, he formed a government with members from different political parties (a <u>coalition</u>). He convinced his government not to negotiate with Germany, but to continue to <u>fight</u> and never surrender.

© Walter Stoneman/Getty Images

Winston Churchill

4) British <u>propaganda</u> (information designed to influence how people think) portrayed Churchill as a <u>strong leader</u> who would win the war for Britain.

5) Throughout the war, Churchill made many speeches on the radio. He used speeches to boost the <u>morale</u> of the British people and the armed forces.

The Home Front

During the war, both the <u>government</u> and the <u>public</u> in Britain had to adapt to wartime life. Many measures were introduced to help <u>protect people</u> at home, and to <u>help defeat the Nazis</u>.

The Blitz caused Destruction across Britain

1) Germany bombed London <u>almost nightly</u> between <u>September 1940</u> and <u>May 1941</u> and again between <u>June 1944</u> and <u>March 1945</u>. <u>Industrial areas</u> (<u>factories</u> and <u>docks</u>) and <u>residential areas</u> were both bombed. Tens of thousands were <u>killed</u> and millions were made <u>homeless</u>.

2) Life for Londoners was <u>tough</u> during the Blitz. It could be hard to get hold of <u>food</u>, and gas, electricity and water supplies sometimes <u>failed</u>.

3) Other cities, including Bristol, Manchester, Birmingham and Liverpool, were also bombed. An attack on <u>Coventry</u> on <u>14 November</u> destroyed a third of the city, and <u>killed hundreds</u> of people.

4) However, the Blitz did not achieve its aims. It caused <u>fewer deaths</u> than expected and failed to <u>destroy morale</u> or force Britain to <u>surrender</u>.

Measures were introduced to Protect People

Here are some of the ways in which Britain <u>defended</u> itself against <u>German attacks</u>:

The Blackout

The <u>blackout</u> was designed to <u>stop German pilots</u> from <u>seeing towns and cities</u>. People had to <u>cover their windows</u> at night so that house lights couldn't be seen. <u>Streetlights</u> and <u>car headlights</u> also had to be turned off.

Air Raid Shelters

Many people built <u>Anderson shelters</u> in their gardens. These were shelters made of <u>corrugated iron</u>, often dug into the <u>ground</u>, designed to <u>protect</u> people from bombing.

In London, <u>underground stations</u> were used as air-raid shelters. <u>Thousands of people</u> took cover in them, often taking bedding, food, and games to spend the whole night there.

The Government wanted to Control the Media

1) The <u>Ministry of Information</u> was set up to carry out <u>censorship</u> — controlling what <u>stories</u> and <u>photographs</u> newspapers could print. All <u>post</u> coming in from abroad was opened and read.

2) The Ministry carried out <u>propaganda campaigns</u> to <u>lift morale</u> and to encourage people to help the war effort. A campaign called '<u>Careless Talk Costs Lives</u>' told people not to gossip about the war, and '<u>Dig For Victory</u>' told people to grow their own vegetables.

A poster encouraging people to grow their own food.

Life was very different in Britain during the war...

People had to adapt to huge changes in the 1940s — it was important to keep up morale.

Sources and Questions

These questions will help you really perfect your knowledge of Hitler's rise to power and how the Second World War affected life in Britain.

1 *Germany took control of much of the territory surrounding it in the 1930s.*
This was one of the causes of the Second World War.
Read Sources A to D and then answer the questions below.

Source A — A map of German expansion pre-World War Two

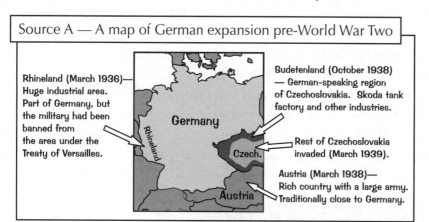

Rhineland (March 1936)— Huge industrial area. Part of Germany, but the military had been banned from the area under the Treaty of Versailles.

Germany

Sudetenland (October 1938) — German-speaking region of Czechoslovakia. Skoda tank factory and other industries.

Rest of Czechoslovakia invaded (March 1939).

Austria (March 1938)— Rich country with a large army. Traditionally close to Germany.

Source B — A Sudeten woman cries as the Nazis arrive.

© Time Life Pictures/Getty Images

Source C — A speech by the Austrian Chancellor, 11th March 1938

The German Government today handed to President Miklas an ultimatum, with a time limit, ordering him to nominate as chancellor a person designated by the German Government and to appoint members of a cabinet on the orders of the German Government. Otherwise German troops would invade Austria.

ultimatum= final demand

designated = decided

Source D — Hitler in a speech on March 25th 1938

Certain foreign newspapers have said that we fell on Austria with brutal methods. I can only say that even in death they cannot stop lying. I have in the course of my political struggle won much love from my people, but when I crossed the former frontier (into Austria) there met me such a stream of love as I have never experienced. Not as tyrants have we come, but as liberators.

a) Look at Source A, then copy and complete this paragraph using phrases from the box below.

The map shows .... expansion before the Second World War. There were many reasons why .... wanted to take control of these areas. They were a good source of .... and military resources, as well as having valuable ....

| Hitler | German | industry | money |

b) Does Source D agree with Source C that the take over of Austria was forced through with threats? Explain your answer.

c) Look at Sources B and C. Do the Sources suggest that German expansion was a popular move? Explain your answer.

Sources and Questions

2 *During World War Two, people in Britain faced new challenges in their daily lives. Read Sources A to C and answer the questions below.*

Source A — Poster from the 1940s

Source B — Blitz damage in London in 1941

© Hudson/Getty Images

Source C — Part of a speech by Winston Churchill given in the House of Commons, 4th June 1940

"We shall not flag or fail. We shall go on to the end... We shall defend our island, whatever the cost may be. We shall fight on the beaches, we shall fight on the landing-grounds, we shall fight in the fields and in the streets, we shall fight in the hills. We shall never surrender!"

a) Look at Sources A and B. Why did the government think it was a good idea to evacuate children out of London at the start of World War Two?

b) Look at Source C. Which statement below best summarises Churchill's approach to World War Two?

   i) Churchill was pessimistic that Britain would be able to win the war, especially during the Blitz.

   ii) Churchill was determined to win the war and encouraged people in Britain to keep a fighting spirit.

   iii) Churchill believed that it would be easy for Britain to win the war.

Hitler's Persecution of the Jews

Anti-semitism wasn't new, it had been in evidence since medieval times — but Hitler's anti-semitism was far more extreme than anything that had come before.

Hitler created a **Totalitarian State**

When Adolf Hitler and the Nazis came to power in 1933, they created a totalitarian state. Human rights were not important to Hitler.

1) Political prisoners were held in concentration camps.

2) Hitler tried to "purify" German blood by locking up gypsies, homosexuals, alcoholics and the mentally and physically handicapped in concentration camps.

3) Many of these people were systematically killed.

4) However it was the Jews who Hitler was particularly keen to eliminate.

> A totalitarian state is where the government has complete control of a country. The people have no say in how it's run.
>
> The government controls the press and there's no freedom of speech. Human rights are usually lost by many citizens.

Hitler hated the **Jews**

Jews were seen by Hitler as a very distinct social group. He held them responsible for Germany's problems.

1) During his rise to power, Hitler blamed the Jews for Germany's economic problems and defeat in World War I.

2) He used his storm troopers, called the SA, to stir up hatred towards the Jews.

3) Hitler used propaganda in newspapers and newsreels to increase the hatred towards Jews.

> Propaganda is information (sometimes invented) presented in a way that is meant to influence and manipulate people's way of thinking.

Hitler's storm troopers

© Hudson/Getty Images

The SA (Sturm-Abteilung) was Hitler's private army. Formed in 1921, by the early 1930s it contained over 4 million men.

Led by Ernst Röhm, the men were given free shirts and meals. They were often called the 'Brown Shirts' because of their brown uniform.

Hitler used them to hand out Nazi propaganda, protect Nazi meetings, and as thugs to beat up opponents of the Nazis.

In 1938 Hitler got rid of the SA and replaced them with the SS (Schutzstaffel).

Totalitarianism means there's no freedom of speech...

That means that people who speak out against the government get arrested, or worse. So if you're being persecuted, there's not really much you can do about it.

Hitler's Persecution of the Jews

The Jews were Gradually Persecuted

When he came to power Hitler began to systematically persecute the Jews.

1) After he came to power, attacks on Jews increased. Jews were banned from professional jobs in such things as medicine and law.

2) In 1935, the Nuremberg Laws banned Jews from marrying non-Jews. The Reich Citizenship Laws removed their right to vote and their protection by the law.

3) By 1938, the Jews were banned from public places.

4) On the Night of Broken Glass (Kristallnacht) Jewish shops and synagogues were smashed. Over 20,000 Jewish men were sent to concentration camps.

> Concentration camps were a British invention, used during the Boer War at the beginning of the 20th century. They were a way of locking up enemies of the state, usually in poor conditions resulting in a high death rate.

© Mary Evans Picture Library

A Jewish shop in Berlin in the 1930s.

This picture is typical of what happened to Jewish shops in Germany after the Nazis started a campaign to get people to avoid Jewish businesses.

Jews were also made to wear the star of David on their clothes, so that everyone could tell if someone was a Jew.

Timeline of Hitler's Persecution of the Jews

1933	Mass persecution began with the boycott of Jewish shops and businesses.
1935	Reich Citizenship Laws.
1935	Nuremberg Laws.
1938	Kristallnacht, Night of Broken Glass.
1938	Jews banned from public places.
1939	Jews captured in Poland were shut up into ghettos such as Warsaw, in appalling conditions.

Written Source — 1938

"The day after Kristallnacht the teachers told us 'don't worry about what you see, even if you see some nasty things which you may not understand. Hitler wants a better Germany, a clean Germany. Don't worry everything will work out fine in the end.'" *Henrik Metelmann, a member of the Hitler Youth, explaining how he was told that bad things happening to Jews was OK.*

Ghettos Created by the Nazis

A ghetto is an area of a city where members of a particular racial group live, usually in poor living conditions. In 1940 the Nazis gave it a more sinister meaning.

The Jews had to live in **Ghettos**

1) Originally, the Nazis were going to create a <u>reservation</u> for Jews near <u>Lublin</u> in <u>Poland</u>.

2) However, they quickly <u>changed their minds</u> and started to <u>wall off</u> areas of cities to house the Jews.

3) These areas were called <u>ghettos</u> — the <u>biggest</u> was in <u>Warsaw</u>.

4) Conditions in these overcrowded slums were <u>terrible</u>, with <u>hundreds of thousands</u> dying.

Ghettos In Occupied Poland

Warsaw
Lodz
Lublin
Krakow

Germany   Poland 1939 Border
Soviet Union   • Ghetto

Conditions in the Ghetto

Whole families were crowded into each room. The Jews were given a handful of bread each day. If they tried to leave the ghetto they were murdered. Diseases like dysentery and typhus killed those people already weakened by hunger.

Many German people didn't know about the conditions in the ghettos. They were shown newsreels of Jews being resettled in good conditions.

Part of the reason Hitler began invading countries in Eastern Europe was for 'living space' — he thought Germany was overpopulated and needed more land to expand and grow more food.

The **Germans** took **Holland** in **May 1940**

1) The Germans took control of <u>Amsterdam</u> and the rest of <u>Holland</u> in <u>May 1940</u>.

2) The <u>Jews</u> living in <u>Holland</u> were soon made to live under <u>similar rules</u> to the German Jews.

3) Many Jews were <u>deported to Germany</u> to work in <u>forced labour camps</u>. Many <u>disappeared</u>.

Written Source — 1922

"If I am ever really in power the destruction of the Jews will be my first and most important job. As soon as I have the power, I shall have gallows after gallows erected... Then the Jews will be hanged one after another... until Germany is cleansed of the last Jew." *Part of a letter written by Hitler to Josef Hell. It shows that Hitler had been thinking about how to deal with the 'Jewish problem' years before he came to power.*

Anne Frank

Many Jewish people were unable to escape from Nazi occupied countries, so instead they hid, hoping they wouldn't be found...

The **Franks** were a **Jewish Family** who Hid from the Nazis

The Frank family were <u>Jewish</u>. They originally lived in <u>Germany</u> but then moved to <u>Amsterdam</u> to get away from the Nazis. Then the Nazis invaded the Netherlands. They began to <u>round up Jews</u> and sent them to labour camps or concentration camps. In <u>July 1942</u>, Otto Frank took his family into <u>hiding</u> in a building attached to his office. His daughter Anne kept a <u>diary</u> of the events.

1) Some <u>brave friends</u> brought them <u>food</u> and kept the hiding place secret.

2) The Franks stayed in the secret annexe until <u>1944</u>, when the <u>allied liberating forces</u> were <u>close by</u>. Another Jewish family, the Van Pels, and a family friend, Fritz Pfeffer, also hid in the annexe with the Franks.

3) But the annexe was <u>raided by the SS</u> on 4th August 1944 and the inhabitants were <u>all</u> sent to <u>concentration camps</u>.

4) Anne and her sister Margot died within a few days of each other in <u>Bergen-Belsen</u> concentration camp, about a month before the camp was liberated by the allies. Of the eight people who lived in the annexe, Otto Frank was the only survivor.

5) Anne's diary was found by the family's friends, who gave it to Otto when he returned. Otto Frank published the diary in <u>1947</u>.

Anne Frank's diary was published in 1947. It was translated into English in 1951 and has sold millions of copies, helping publicise the horror of the Holocaust.

The house where Anne's family hid is now a museum.

Photo of Anne Frank in May 1942, just two months before she went into hiding.

© Anne Frank Fonds Basel/Getty Images

Anne Frank was 13 years old when she went into hiding...

The people in the secret annexe hid there for over two years — just imagine... You couldn't go outside at all and you were living in constant fear that you would be found.

The Final Solution

For Hitler it wasn't enough to make all the Jews live in ghettos, he wanted to get rid of them completely. The Final Solution was his plan to kill all the Jews.

The Einsatzgruppen Shot many Jews

The first Jews to be murdered were the Polish and Russian Jews.
They were murdered by special units of the SS called Einsatzgruppen.

1) At first Jews were taken out and made to dig their own graves before being shot.

2) Thousands of men, women and children were shot in this way.

3) Then the Nazis decided they wanted to speed up this process.

4) The Nazis started to build death camps at places such as Treblinka and Auschwitz-Birkenau.

5) Many Jews were moved to the ghettos at places such as Lodz and Warsaw where they were kept until the death camps were ready.

The Final Solution began in March 1942

In March 1942, the Final Solution began in earnest at Auschwitz-Birkenau.

1) Auschwitz-Birkenau was a dual purpose camp — Auschwitz was a labour camp, but Birkenau was an extermination camp.

2) On their arrival by train, the Jews were divided into two groups — those fit to work (although they were virtually worked to death), and those unfit to work (like children or the elderly) who would be killed straight away.

3) Those chosen to die were calmly told to undress. They were shaved and told they were going to have a shower. Once in the shower, they were killed with Zyklon B, a poisonous gas.

4) The bodies were then cremated after gold teeth had been pulled out and jewellery removed.

Concentration camps were where Germans sent Jews, Gypsies, political and religious opponents and other 'undesirables'. People weren't systematically killed in these camps but many were forced to work and thousands died from starvation, disease and maltreatment.

Extermination camps were where the Nazis carried out mass murder using gas chambers.

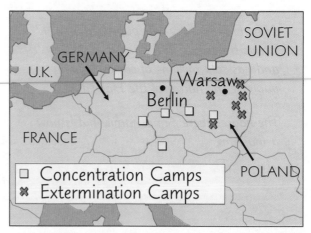

Written Source — 1947-9

"At Auschwitz I used Zyklon B, a crystallised prussic acid dropped into the death chamber. It took from three to fifteen minutes to kill the people in the chamber. We knew they were dead when the screaming stopped. After the bodies were removed, soldiers took off their rings and extracted the gold from their teeth. We built our gas chambers to take 2000 at one time."
The Commandant of the Auschwitz extermination camp speaking about the camp at the Nuremberg trials. The Nuremberg trials took place between 1947-1949.

The Final Solution

*The **Final Solution** led to the murder of over **Six Million** people*

In 1945, Allied soldiers began to <u>liberate the camps</u> and could not believe the horror they found.

1) The Allied solders were overwhelmed by the scenes of death and near death they witnessed.

2) <u>Over six million</u> people had been <u>murdered</u> mechanically by the Nazi regime — Jews, gypsies, political prisoners, homosexuals, handicapped people and prisoners of war were all victims of the Nazis.

3) Many of the Germans who had run the death camps were brought to justice at the <u>Nuremberg Trials</u> after the war.

4) Hitler <u>shot himself</u> on 30 April 1945 in a bunker in Berlin.

As the Allied troops defeated the Germans and pushed into Nazi territory, the Nazis tried to destroy some of the concentration camps. They marched the prisoners to different camps. But eventually they just gave up, so the Allied troops were able to liberate prisoners from the camps the Nazis had left.

One of the men in this photo is Elie Wiesel (7th from the left on the middle bunk next to the vertical post). He went on to become an internationally famous writer and academic — he won the Nobel Prize for Peace in 1986.

© H. Miller/Getty Images

Prisoners of the Buchenwald concentration camp. This photo was taken when the camp was liberated by the American troops.

*Some people **Deny** the **Holocaust** happened*

Over the years there have been lots of different responses to the Holocaust.

1) Some people try to pretend it <u>didn't happen</u>.

2) Some people have concluded that there is <u>no God</u>, or that if there is one, he doesn't care about us.

3) Other people use it as a <u>lesson</u>, to promote kindness and to try to make sure that it never ever happens again.

4) Auschwitz-Birkenau has been turned into a museum and memorial. Over 25 million people have visited it.

Over 6 million people died in concentration camps...

It's scary to think that the idea of the Final Solution and the murder of millions of people came from just one man — it shows how bad a totalitarian state can be.

Sources and Questions

Hitler and the Final Solution is a really nasty piece of history, but a good historian must always try to treat each source with an open mind — even if the sources you are using are biased.

1   In Eastern Europe, Jews were separated from other people and imprisoned in ghettos by the Nazis. Read Sources A and B, then answer the questions below.

Source A — A survivor remembers the Vilna ghetto

As we entered, we were directed to a house that would have been occupied by a family of four to six people under normal conditions — now 25 or 30 of us were crammed in. Everybody was searching for a place to sleep... Going to the synagogue, praying and studying about our religion were absolutely forbidden. The Germans wanted to break the Jewish spirit and morale. Many people lost their will to live, but I was too stubborn to give in.

ghetto = a walled off area of a city where Jews were forced to live by the Nazis.

Source B — Polish Police official, Krakow District, 1941

There was great hatred against the Jews. It was revenge, and they [the police] wanted money and gold. Don't let's kid ourselves, there was always something up for grabs during the Jewish actions. Everywhere you went there was something for the asking.

a) Read Source A. Describe two ways in which Jews were mistreated in the ghetto.

b) What explanation does Source A give for the treatment of the Jews?

c) According to Source B, why were members of the police prepared to take part in "actions" against the Jews?

2   Anne Frank and her family hid from the Nazis in Amsterdam from 1942 until 1944, when they were betrayed. Anne and her family were deported to concentration camps. Anne and her sister Margot both died at Bergen-Belsen concentration camp.

Source A — A description of Bergen-Belsen concentration camp

Margot and Anne were transferred to Bergen-Belsen where they both died due to the terrible conditions there. Bergen-Belsen did not have gas chambers but there was extreme overcrowding, and mass deaths occurred as a direct result of planned starvation and epidemics such as typhus. Anne and Margot, like so many other inmates, would have had little food, clothing, or medicine. As the Allies moved closer, the German military began dismantling the camps and conditions for the inmates deteriorated even further.

gas chambers = poisonous gas was used to murder people in the death camps.

a) Write down two reasons for the mass deaths at Bergen-Belsen concentration camp.

b) Using the information in Source A, describe what conditions were like in the camp for Anne and Margot in your own words.

Sources and Questions

3 *The Nazis persecuted several different groups of people, including Jews, the Roma (gypsies), homosexuals and political opponents. Read Source A, then answer the questions below.*

Source A — The persecution of the Roma

Nazi scientists regarded the Roma as an inferior race. Therefore they believed the Roma could never be taught how to be good Germans. In 1935 they were classified as 'aliens' and so were subject to the Nuremberg Laws, along with the Jews. In October 1939, the Roma were sent to concentration camps in the newly conquered Poland. Then, in 1942 all the Roma were taken to a special gypsy camp which was part of the Auschwitz-Birkenau concentration camp in Poland. In 1944 the Russian army advanced towards the camp. The SS shot all the Roma before leaving. In total it is thought that the Nazis murdered over 200,000 of the Roma during the war.

a) Why did the Nazis persecute the Roma, according to Source A?

b) Use Source A to draw a timeline of the treatment of the Roma by the Nazis from 1935-1944.

4 *Many Nazi leaders held responsible for the death camps were tried and executed after the war. Study Sources A and B, then answer the questions below.*

Source A — The trial of the Nazi Adolf Eichmann

© Getty Images

Adolf Eichmann carried out and coordinated the 'final solution'

Source B — The trial of Adolf Eichmann described by a modern historian

alleged war criminals = people suspected of committing war crimes

Alleged war criminals were being brought to trial long after the end of World War II. In 1960 the Nazi official Adolf Eichmann... was kidnapped by Israeli agents and taken to Jerusalem to be tried as a war criminal. He was tried and condemned the following year and executed in 1962.

a) What can you learn from Source A about how those responsible for the death camps were treated after the Second World War was over? Choose either i) or ii) as your answer.

i) Source A shows that the people responsible for the death camps were put on trial for their war crimes. Photographs are useful as evidence — they show a lot of information.

ii) Source A shows that at least one of the people responsible for the death camps was put on trial. Photographs are limited as evidence — they leave out a lot of information.

b) What further information does Source B give about what happened to Eichmann after the war?

Indian Independence

India became part of the British Empire in 1858 (p. 82). Indian resources made the Empire a lot of money, but there were some Indians who wanted independence. After World War One, the independence movement grew stronger.

There was **Discontent** amongst the **Indian Population**

Britain benefited from having India as a colony. It was good for <u>trade</u>, provided <u>millions of troops</u> and <u>workers</u> in World War One and Two and was a source of <u>pride</u> for Britain.

Advantages of British rule

1) Britain helped India to <u>modernise</u> by building railways and improving the schooling system.
2) The British also <u>revolutionised</u> Indian industry. Production of <u>tea</u>, <u>coffee</u> and <u>spices</u>, as well as other manufacturing processes, provided jobs.

However — many Indians wanted to be <u>independent</u> from British rule. Britain had brought problems to India, as well as benefits.

Disadvantages of British rule

1) Britain imposed <u>harsh taxes</u> on India. This meant that whilst most people had jobs, many were <u>living in poverty</u> and couldn't afford to support themselves and their families.
2) Most of the money coming into India went to the British. There were very few Indian <u>landowners</u> and most big business was British-owned. The employees of these companies were often treated <u>terribly</u>, and were thought of as easy and cheap to replace.
3) India had no independence. The British installed loyal governments and anyone who <u>rejected</u> British rule was treated <u>harshly</u>.

There was **Religious Tension** in India

1) There were <u>three</u> main religious groups in India — Hindus, Muslims and Sikhs. But they didn't always get along — even before the British arrived.
2) The British often made the division worse by following a policy of 'divide and rule'. This meant empowering the <u>Hindus</u>, and ignoring the <u>Muslims</u> in the day-to-day running of the country.
3) The British established a democratically-elected <u>Indian National Congress (INC)</u>. However it was always clear that whilst Indians could have a small say in the running of their country they were very much under <u>British Rule</u>. The <u>INC</u> eventually became more active in calling for Indian independence. The <u>two main Indian political parties</u> in the INC were:

The Congress Party

- Mainly Hindu.
- <u>Gandhi</u> was a key member.
- Wanted India to remain <u>united</u>, with better rights under British rule.
- Later split into '<u>hot</u>' faction, who wanted revolution — and '<u>soft</u>' faction, who wanted peace.

The Muslim League

- A <u>Muslim</u> party.
- They wanted India to be <u>independent</u> from British rule.
- They wanted to divide India into <u>two</u> <u>states</u> — one <u>Hindu</u> and one <u>Muslim</u>.

Indian Independence

The British *Couldn't Stop* the *Independence Movement*

Living conditions for Indian people were getting <u>worse</u> in the early 20th century, and the British weren't seen to be <u>helping</u>. Calls for independence began to <u>grow</u>. Led by Gandhi, a campaign for <u>civil disobedience</u> began to bring an end to British rule <u>without</u> using <u>violence</u>.

Time Line – Mahatma Gandhi

1869	Mohandas Karamchand Gandhi is born.
1888	Gandhi studies law in Britain.
1891-14	Gandhi spends years in South Africa campaigning for fairer treatment of Indians.
1919	The British shoot into crowds at a peaceful gathering at <u>Amritsar</u>. <u>Hundreds</u> are killed and wounded. Hatred for British rule grows and the '<u>Quit India</u>' movement and Gandhi are increasingly popular.
1920	Gandhi organises a <u>boycott</u> of British goods and institutions.
1922-24	Gandhi is imprisoned by the British.
1930	Gandhi organises the '<u>salt march</u>' — thousands march to the sea to make salt in protest of the British taxes on it.
1931	Gandhi tries to negotiate for Indian independence in London but fails.
1947	India and Pakistan are granted independence as separate countries. Gandhi is pleased with independence but opposed to the <u>partition</u> — he wants a <u>united India</u>.
1948	Gandhi is assassinated by a Hindu fanatic. After his death he becomes known as '<u>Mahatma</u>' meaning 'great soul'. His approach of peaceful protest is influential on later campaigners including <u>Martin Luther King</u>.

© Mary Evans Picture Library

Gandhi

India's problems *Didn't End* with independence

When the British granted India <u>independence</u> in <u>1947</u>, they left without setting up a workable <u>government</u> for the country. Violence erupted between <u>Hindus</u> and <u>Muslims</u>, both of whom wanted <u>power</u> in the new country. It was decided to <u>divide</u> India in two.

1) <u>Pakistan</u> — would be mostly <u>Muslim</u>. It declared independence on <u>August 14 1947</u>.

2) <u>India</u> — would be mostly <u>Hindu</u> and <u>Sikh</u>. It declared independence on <u>August 15 1947</u>.

The two countries were British <u>Dominions</u> — they still had the <u>British king or queen</u>.

1) In <u>1950</u> India became a republic — the British queen was no longer the Head of State.

2) In <u>1971</u> Pakistan did the same thing.

3) In 1971 a <u>civil war</u> in <u>Pakistan</u> resulted in a further split. <u>Bangladesh</u> was created.

Indian independence came at a high price...

Millions of people died or were displaced in the struggle to win independence for India and Pakistan. The two countries still fight today over the disputed region of Kashmir in the North.

Egyptian Independence and the Suez Crisis

Access to the Suez Canal in Egypt prompted a crisis in 1956.

Britain had a lot of Influence in Egypt

1) Throughout the 19th century, Britain <u>invested</u> heavily in Egypt. In 1875, Britain bought a large number of shares in the <u>Suez Canal</u>, which Egypt was selling in order to <u>raise money</u> to pay off its debts.

2) Access to the canal was <u>really important</u> to Britain, who used it for transporting <u>oil</u> and other goods to and from <u>India</u> and the rest of the <u>British Empire</u> in Asia and East Africa.

3) Britain wanted to <u>increase its control</u> over Egyptian affairs in order to protect its investments. In 1882, Britain used <u>military force</u> to invade Egypt. Britain continued to rule the country until 1922.

4) In 1922 Britain agreed to Egyptian <u>independence</u>, but maintained a strong presence in the country into the 1950s.

5) After <u>World War Two</u>, there was a greater demand in Egypt for the British to leave. The government that came to power in 1954 said they would <u>end British influence</u> in Egypt.

A map showing the Suez Canal

The Suez Crisis took place in 1956

1) In 1956, the Egyptian president, Gamal Abdel Nasser, announced the <u>nationalisation</u> of the <u>Suez Canal</u>. This was against the interests of Britain and France who relied on it for <u>shipping goods</u>, especially <u>oil</u>.

2) British Prime Minister <u>Anthony Eden</u> took part in negotiations to hold on to the Suez Canal, but no agreement was reached.

3) Britain, France and Israel held <u>secret talks</u> planning a military <u>invasion</u> of Egypt in order to regain control of the canal. In October 1956, Israel invaded Egypt.

4) Shortly afterwards, Britain and France <u>invaded</u> Egypt as well. The United States, the USSR and the United Nations <u>condemned</u> their actions.

5) The US put pressure on the UK and France to <u>withdraw</u> their troops, which they did.

Nationalisation is when a country's government takes control of certain businesses or resources.

Britain's Reputation was Damaged by the Suez Crisis

1) Britain had been <u>embarrassed</u> on a global scale by <u>trying</u> and <u>failing</u> to keep its <u>power</u> in a country that wanted to run its own affairs.

2) The conflict over Suez made Britain unpopular as it appeared <u>old-fashioned</u> and desperate to cling on to its old <u>colonial territories</u>. The conflict encouraged other countries in <u>Africa</u> which still belonged to the British Empire to struggle for <u>independence</u> in the decade after the Suez crisis.

3) Britain and the US's close relationship became temporarily <u>strained</u> by the crisis. Britain had been forced to <u>back down</u> by the US, which showed that Britain was no longer as powerful as it had been in the 1800s.

Another step in the collapse of the British Empire...

After World War Two, it was increasingly clear that Britain could not keep its grip on its territory abroad. Suez was an embarrassing example of how Britain's status was changing.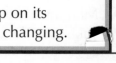

Irish Independence

It wasn't just distant colonies that were fighting for independence in the 20th century...

Ireland had a History of Struggle against England

1) English monarchs including Elizabeth I and James I had taken land from Irish Catholics and given it to Protestants loyal to the crown.

2) The English had used violence to put down Catholic rebellions throughout the 17th century.

3) Laws were passed in Ireland to restrict the freedom of Catholics — discrimination was used as a method of control.

4) The Act of Union in 1800 abolished the status of Ireland as a separate kingdom. Many Catholics resented this loss of independence.

5) There were over one million deaths and mass emigration during the Great Famine of the late 1840s. The British government and landowners did little to help, which caused anger among the Irish.

The Great Famine

The Great Famine was caused by potato blight — a disease that made potatoes rot in the field so they couldn't be eaten. This was a disaster as potatoes were the staple food of over 4 million Irish people at the time.

It is estimated that about 1 million people died of starvation and disease. Thousands more emigrated to Britain, America, Canada and Australia.

There was an Independent Ireland from 1920

1) Charles Stuart Parnell and his Irish Parliamentary Party had been campaigning for Home Rule in Ireland since the 1870s. Home Rule would mean that Ireland would govern itself.

2) The two attempts (in 1886 and in 1893) to pass the Bill through English parliament failed.

3) In 1905, the Irish Republican Brotherhood (IRB) re-formed, with the aim of setting up an independent Irish republic. In the same year, the Nationalist Party, Sinn Fein, was formed.

4) In 1912, Parliament passed a Home Rule bill to give Ireland its own government. Unionists (who wanted to remain part of Great Britain) opposed the bill.

5) Parliament planned to amend the bill, but had to postpone further debates due to the outbreak of World War One.

6) In 1916, the IRB organised the Easter Rising to push for independence. The rising failed and 14 of the leaders were executed.

7) Partition finally took place in 1920 with separate parliaments for Northern and Southern Ireland. David Lloyd George, the British Prime Minister, agreed to the Anglo-Irish Treaty. Signed in 1921, it created an independent Ireland but left the Six Counties of Ulster (with majority Protestant populations) as part of the United Kingdom.

8) Irish Nationalists opposed the split. The Irish Republican Army (IRA) committed violent acts in protest, which continued until the signing of the 1998 Good Friday Agreement.

Unionists

Traditionally, Unionists are mostly Protestant, and want Northern Ireland to remain part of Britain.

Nationalists

Traditionally, Nationalists are mostly Catholic. They want a united Ireland free from British rule.

Sources and Questions

Several countries which were part of the British Empire gained independence in the 20th century.

1 *The greatest figure in Indian independence was Gandhi. He believed that Britain could be made to give up rule over India through peaceful means.*

Source A — Gandhi resists the British — a cartoon from 1933

Source B — Gandhi collects salt — a picture from 1930

GANDHI BREAKING THE SALT LAWS: THE CIVIL DISOBEDIENCE IN INDIA.

© Illustrated London News Ltd/Mary Evans

© Mary Evans Picture Library

Source C — Some of Gandhi's famous sayings

'An eye for an eye makes the whole world blind.'
'There are many causes that I am prepared to die for but no causes that I am prepared to kill for.'

a) Describe what Source A shows. Why are the elephant's tusks blunt?

b) Describe in your own words what the first saying in Source C means.

c) Source B shows Gandhi after he led a march to the sea to collect natural salt (the British had put a large tax on salt). What was he trying to achieve?

2 *In 1947 India got independence. But the main religious groups began to fight with one another, and it was decided India had to be separated into India and Pakistan.*

Source A — A modern account of the partition of India

Gandhi wanted Muslims, Hindus and Sikhs to live together — but it was decided to split (partition) India. India and Pakistan would be separate, to keep the religions apart. Over 7 million Hindus and Sikhs moved to India from Pakistan, and about the same number of Muslims moved to Pakistan from India.

Source B — A map of the new India and Pakistan after partition

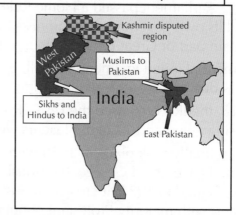

a) Using Source A, which three religious groups were affected by the partition of India?

b) Look at Sources A and B. People of which religion would mainly live in Pakistan?

c) What is unusual about the new Pakistan?

Sources and Questions

3 *In 1956, Britain and France invaded Egypt in order to secure rights to the Suez Canal. Their military action prompted international outcry.*

Source A — A cartoon showing Britain and France at the Suez Canal

Study Source A. What do you think the illustrator's attitude was towards the Suez crisis?

---

4 *In 1920, the British government divided the mostly Catholic south and the mostly Protestant north of Ireland into two countries. This was called partition. Partition provoked violence on both sides. Read Source A, then answer the questions below.*

Source A — Violence in Ireland, described by a modern historian

On 21 November 1920... Collins sent his men to break into the homes or hotel rooms of fourteen British agents and kill them in cold blood. Within hours the Black and Tans reacted by firing into a crowd of about 8000 spectators at a Gaelic football match.

Collins = Michael Collins, head of the Irish Republican Army (IRA)

Black and Tans = British police in Ireland

a) Give one example of violence in Source A that was:
   i)   carefully planned.
   ii) revenge.

b) Which of the following statements best describes Source A?
   i)   Source A seems biased because the author is defending the IRA's actions.
   ii) Source A seems biased because the author is agreeing with the actions of the British agents.
   iii) Source A seems unbiased as it is condemning the actions of both the IRA and the British.

The Welfare State — The Liberal Reforms

In the early 20th century, many people in Britain were living in poverty. Politicians began to make changes to improve their situation. This was the beginning of the welfare state.

Many **Poor People** lived in **Terrible Conditions**

1) At the start of the 20th century, many poor people in large, industrial cities lived in <u>slums</u>. Slums were areas of poor accommodation, with <u>no running water</u> or proper <u>sewerage</u>. Large families often shared just one room and <u>diseases</u> spread easily.

2) People worked <u>long hours</u> for <u>low pay</u>. If they were made <u>unemployed</u> or became <u>too old</u> to work, there were no benefits or pensions to help them. The only help was <u>workhouses</u> run by local councils. Here, people were given basic food and a bed in return for working long hours in tough conditions.

3) When the Boer War broke out in 1899, <u>40%</u> of volunteers were rejected. This was mostly due to <u>health problems</u> related to poverty including <u>poor diet</u> and <u>living conditions</u>.

Children in a London slum in the early 1900s.

A **Royal Commission** investigated **Poverty**

In <u>1905</u> the <u>Conservative</u> government set up a <u>Royal Commission</u> to look at whether they should give more help to the poor. Members of the Commission <u>couldn't agree</u> about what <u>caused</u> poverty so they published <u>two reports</u>:

The Majority Report	The Minority Report
(what the majority of the commission thought)	(what the minority of the commission thought)
• The poor made themselves poor by <u>gambling</u> and <u>drinking</u> — so they didn't deserve help.	• Poverty was caused by things like <u>illness</u>, <u>old age</u> and a <u>shortage of jobs</u>.
• Enough was being done for the poor <u>already</u>.	• They thought <u>more should be done</u> to prevent people being poor.

After **1906** the **Liberals** brought in **Social Reforms**

1) In <u>1906</u> the Liberal Party came to power. They were influenced by the <u>Minority Report</u> and pressure from the <u>general public</u> to bring in <u>laws</u> to deal with poverty.

2) The <u>poor health</u> of volunteers for the Boer War had been a shock. If Britain was involved in a <u>major war</u>, it would need a <u>healthy people</u> to fight as soldiers.

3) The <u>Labour Party</u> had been founded recently and was gathering a lot of support from the working classes. The Liberals wanted to keep <u>working class votes</u> by showing that they would help the poor too.

4) Two MPs, <u>David Lloyd George</u> and <u>Winston Churchill</u>, worked hard to drive the welfare bills through. They wanted to <u>help the poor</u>, but were also keen to <u>make a name for themselves</u>.

The Welfare State — The Liberal Reforms

The Liberals also passed laws to help working people, the elderly and children.

Children were given Special Protection

1) In 1906, the government brought in the School Meals Act. This allowed local councils to raise taxes to provide free school meals for the poorest children.

2) In 1907, children started receiving free medical inspections at school.

3) In 1908, Parliament passed the Children and Young Persons' Act, also known as the Children's Charter. This made it a crime for parents or carers to beat or neglect their children. It also became illegal to send children out begging or to make them carry out dangerous work.

4) The Charter also made it illegal for children younger than 16 to buy cigarettes or go into pubs.

Elderly people got State Pensions

1) Many old people were very poor. If they couldn't work they had no income.

2) In 1908 Lloyd George introduced the Old Age Pensions Act. The pension was for people over 70 on low incomes. People who were well off didn't qualify for a state pension.

3) The pensions were paid for by money raised through ordinary taxes but it was an incredibly popular policy.

More Help was given to Workers

1) In 1909, the Liberal government introduced a minimum wage for workers.

2) It also set up labour exchanges. Labour exchanges were like job centres, where unemployed workers could go to find out about job vacancies.

3) Within five years there was a network of labour exchanges right across Britain. One million jobs a year were filled through the exchanges.

The National Insurance Act of 1911 introduced Benefits

1) In 1911 Lloyd George introduced the National Insurance Act.

2) Workers, employers and the government all paid into a scheme which then gave financial help to workers when they were too ill to work.

3) It also brought in unemployment benefit for workers in shipbuilding, iron founding and construction. These were industries where workers were often out of work for long periods.

4) Employers, employees and the government paid into an unemployment fund and in return, workers were paid unemployment benefits for up to 15 weeks a year.

The beginning of the welfare state...

It's hard to imagine what life was like before sick-pay and pensions, but these things that we take for granted today were pretty radical when they were introduced in the early 1900s.

The Welfare State — The NHS

The creation of the NHS was a great achievement of the post-war government.

The **Welfare State** stalled after **World War One**

1) After the First World War, the government promised to make Britain a land "fit for heroes". However, the First World War had drained Britain's resources.

2) During the 1930s, the global depression (see p. 116-118) made things worse. The government had to cut back on spending on welfare.

People wanted **Change** after **World War Two**

1) The Second World War had forced people from different backgrounds to work together. In the army, powerful people noticed that the poor had more health problems. Families who took in evacuees from London also realised how disadvantaged many people were.

2) During the Blitz of 1940, the government had provided free treatment to air raid casualties. This had been very successful and very popular.

3) After the Second World War people wanted to improve society and prevent anyone returning to the poverty of the 1930s. It was these feelings that led to Labour winning the election in 1945.

The **Beveridge Report** led to the creation of the **NHS**

Sir William Beveridge published his famous Beveridge Report in 1942. In it he called for the state provision of social security "from the cradle to the grave". He argued that all people should have the right to be free from want (poverty), disease, ignorance, squalor (slum housing) and idleness (unemployment). He called these the five "giants".

1) In 1948, the Labour government introduced the National Health Service (the NHS).

2) It would give everyone the right to visit a doctor, dentist or optician for free. The NHS would provide free medicine and treatment.

3) The NHS guaranteed that hospitals would receive money from the government. Before the NHS they had to rely on charities for money.

Who opposed the NHS?

- Many Conservatives opposed the NHS. They believed it would be too expensive.

- Many doctors opposed it too. They wanted to continue being independent professionals, and not be controlled by the government. They felt the NHS was the government interfering between doctors and patients.

- Some doctors also worried that they would earn less working through the NHS.

The **NHS** was **Popular**, but **Expensive**

1) The NHS proved to be hugely popular. More people than expected accessed the service and by 1950 the NHS was costing twice as much as originally estimated.

2) To cope with the rising costs, some fees, including prescription charges, were introduced in 1951.

British Society 1950s-1960s

For many people in Britian, the 1950s saw a rise in the standard of living.

There was a **Housing Crisis** after **World War Two**

1) Housing was a priority after World War Two. Bombing had destroyed many homes, and there were still people living in poor-quality slum housing.

2) The government made plans for large-scale housing developments. The New Towns Act in 1946 led to several new towns being built, including Stevenage, Milton Keynes and Basildon.

3) The design of these new towns aimed to be very modern, incorporating green spaces and shopping centres. They also contained a large amount of council housing.

4) Another solution to the housing shortage was pre-fabricated housing. 'Prefabs', as they were known, were partly built in factories so that they would be very quick to put up. They were designed to be a temporary solution to the housing problem, though many people lived in them for the rest of their lives.

More **People** had **Access** to **New Technology**

1) Domestic appliances, which had previously been considered luxuries, became more affordable. Ownership of refrigerators, washing machines and vacuum cleaners increased in the 1950s and 1960s.

2) More people owned televisions. Millions of people watched the broadcast of Elizabeth II's coronation in 1953.

3) Car ownership also increased. In 1950 there were fewer than 2 million private cars in Britain. By 1969 there were nearly 10 million.

A family in the 1950s watching television.

© Douglas Miller/Getty Images

Popular Culture was important in the 1950s and 1960s

1) The word teenager became commonly used in the 1950s. Teenagers in the 1950s generally had a better education and more money than any previous generation.

2) Many teenagers spent their money on entertainment — going to the cinema, going dancing and buying fashionable clothes and music records.

3) In the 1950s, 'rock'n'roll' arrived from the USA. Singers such as Elvis Presley and Buddy Holly became popular among young people.

4) Pop culture was really important in the 1960s too. The decade was known as the 'swinging sixties' because of the adventurous new trends among young people.

5) British pop groups like the Beatles and the Who became world-famous. In 1967, the BBC launched Radio 1 to broadcast music to a young audience.

6) Fashion was also revolutionary. Fashion designer Mary Quant helped make the mini-skirt popular, but it caused scandal among older generations in the 1960s.

7) Carnaby Street in London became a centre for fashion and was sometimes thought of as the centre of 'Swinging London'.

British Society 1950s-1960s

After the end of World War Two in 1945, Britain had a shortage of workers. Immigrants, mostly from former colonies in the West Indies and South Asia, came to take up these jobs.

Immigrants *arrived from the* Caribbean

A family arrive in Britain from Jamaica in the 1950s.

© Paul Popper/Popperfoto/Getty Images

1) In 1948, a ship called the Empire Windrush bought over 400 Caribbean migrants to live and work in the UK. Many Caribbean countries were part of the British Commonwealth and most of the immigrants had fought for Britain during World War Two.

2) This marked the start of a period of high immigration of citizens from British Commonwealth countries. By 1961 there were over 100,000 Caribbean people living in London.

3) The types of jobs the Windrush immigrants did tended to be low skilled — e.g. porters, street cleaners, factory workers and builders. Many joined the new NHS and worked for London Transport.

4) Many black immigrants to Britain became victims of prejudice and racism. They were often refused accommodation or service in bars and restaurants.

5) Racism was worst in areas where immigrant communities were largest. In some of these areas, gangs of racist white men would harass members of the black community.

| The Notting Hill Race Riots |

- Openly racist violence came to a head in the summer of 1958. Rioting in Notting Hill, London, lasted for a week. Gangs of white youths threw petrol bombs and glass bottles at homes and businesses owned by immigrants from the Caribbean.

- The events of Notting Hill shocked the British public. In 1965, the Race Relations Act was passed. This made it unlawful to discriminate against people in public places because of their race or nationality. However, racism and racist attacks continued.

Immigrants *also came from* South Asia

1) When India gained independence in 1947, the country was divided into India and Pakistan (see p. 137). 8 million Muslims and 8 million Sikhs and Hindus were forced to leave their homes by the partition.

2) In 1961, there were nearly 190,000 Indian and Pakistani nationals living in Britain.

3) Many came to work in the newly formed NHS as trained doctors. Others worked in the industrial British cities such as Sheffield and Birmingham.

4) Many immigrants were met with discrimination. Enoch Powell, a controversial MP, was angry about the welfare benefits immigrant communities were getting. In his famous 'Rivers of Blood' speech in 1968 he claimed that white British people:

> "…found themselves made strangers in their own country. They found their wives unable to obtain hospital beds in childbirth, their children unable to obtain school places, their homes and neighbourhoods changed beyond recognition, their plans and prospects for the future defeated; [...] they began to hear, as time went by, more and more voices which told them that they were now the unwanted."

British Society 1970s

The 1970s were a time of economic and political problems in Britain.

Strikes in the 1970s affected Daily Life

1) The British economy began to struggle in the 1970s.

2) Old industries, such as mining and shipbuilding, were doing badly. They weren't able to compete with foreign countries that produced the same goods more cheaply.

3) A global oil crisis in 1973 meant there was a shortage of fuel. This was made worse in Britain when coal miners refused to work overtime unless they got a pay rise. The government introduced a three-day working week between January and March 1974 in order to save fuel.

Nurses on strike in 1974.

4) By 1976 the economy was doing so badly that the government had to ask for a large loan from the International Monetary Fund, and make huge spending cuts.

5) The winter of 1978-79 was known as the 'winter of discontent'. Fed up with low pay, many public sector workers went on strike. These included NHS workers, refuse collectors and even some grave-diggers.

6) These problems made the Labour government look very weak, and in 1979 the Conservatives were voted in, under their leader Margaret Thatcher.

> **Effects of the Strikes**
>
> - Power cuts were common. People had to study and work by candlelight.
> - Bakers went on strike, so people had to bake their own bread.
> - The refuse collectors' strike meant that rubbish was piled up in the streets for weeks.

Feminists wanted more Equality

1) At the start of the 1970s, women were expected to carry out the traditional roles of wife and mother. Even if a woman had gone to university, she was expected to give up work and focus on raising children once she was married.

2) During the 1970s, more women in Britain began to challenge these traditional views and inequalities.

3) In 1970, a group of feminists held a protest at the Miss World competition at the Royal Albert Hall. They believed that a female beauty pageant judged by men made women seem like objects.

4) Women who stayed in work were often paid less than men for doing the same job. The 1970 Equal Pay Act made it illegal to pay men more than women doing the same work.

5) The Sex Discrimination Act of 1975 made it illegal to discriminate against someone on the grounds of their sex or marital status.

The 1970s also saw changes in British money...

In 1971, Britain changed its money. It went from a system of pounds, shillings and pence, to having 100 pence to £1 (which we still use today). The process was called decimalisation.

British Society 1980s-1990s

The 1980s and 1990s saw huge social and economic changes in Britain. Throughout the 1980s, the Prime Minister was Margaret Thatcher, a powerful but controversial figure.

Margaret Thatcher was Britain's first Female Prime Minister

1) Margaret Thatcher was leader of the Conservative Party from 1975 to 1990. She became Britain's <u>first female Prime Minister</u> in 1979.

2) Her main aims were to control the power of the <u>trade unions</u> and to boost Britain's <u>economy</u>.

3) <u>Old industries</u>, such as mining, were losing money. Thatcher believed they should be closed down.

4) There was large scale <u>unemployment</u> while she was Prime Minister — over 3 million people were out of work by 1983. This was due to a combination of her <u>policies</u> and a <u>recession</u> from 1980.

5) However, many modern businesses did well from her policies, becoming more <u>productive</u> and <u>competitive</u>.

Margaret Thatcher in 1983.

Society Changed Dramatically in the 1980s and 1990s

The 1980s and 1990s saw <u>dramatic changes</u> in Britain — from family life to the way people work.

Family Structures

1) The 1980s saw the breakdown of <u>traditional family structures</u>.

2) It became more acceptable for couples to live together <u>without being married</u>.

3) Marriage rates fell and <u>divorce rates</u> went up. In the 1990s, around 1 in 3 marriages ended in divorce. People also had <u>fewer children</u>.

Industry and Business

1) In 1900, Britain's economy was based on traditional industries, in particular <u>steelworks</u>, <u>coal mining</u> and <u>ship building</u>.

2) Competition from other countries made these industries uneconomical. <u>New technology</u> also meant that factories could use <u>more machines</u> and <u>fewer people</u>.

3) More and more people began to work in '<u>service</u>' industries. Service industry employees don't make anything — they provide services for other people — for example, in <u>banking</u>, <u>retail</u> and the <u>entertainment industry</u>.

4) In the UK in <u>1961</u>, less that <u>50%</u> of people worked in <u>service</u> industries. By <u>1991</u> that had risen to nearly <u>70%</u> of people.

Technology

1) In the early 1980s, people began buying <u>personal computers</u> to use in homes and businesses. Before then, computers had been so big they took up entire rooms. By the late 1990s, most jobs required a computer in some way.

2) The <u>World Wide Web</u> was launched in 1989 and over the next few decades dramatically changed the way people across the world <u>communicated</u>.

British Society in the 21st Century

Computers have become smaller, more powerful and more widely available.

Communication Technology has Changed the way we Live

Mobile Phones

1) In the 1980s, many people still relied on <u>phone boxes</u> to make calls when they were out.

2) Mobile phones became <u>cheaper</u> as well as <u>lighter</u> throughout the 1990s, and they became increasingly popular. In 2013, <u>94%</u> of adults in Britain owned a mobile phone.

3) Mobile phones are now capable of much more than just making calls. The new generation of '<u>smartphones</u>' are able to connect to the <u>Internet</u>, make <u>video</u> calls, take high-quality <u>photographs</u> and act as a <u>GPS</u> (global positioning system).

4) People use their mobile phones to be <u>constantly connected</u>, and they are able to communicate nearly <u>anywhere in the world</u>. This means that consumers can access online services such as <u>music</u>, <u>banking</u> and <u>retail</u> wherever they are.

© Feverpitched/iStockphotos.com

Touch-screen technology grew in popularity after 2007.

The Internet

1) In <u>2000</u>, around <u>a quarter</u> of British people had access to the Internet. By <u>2010</u> over <u>three quarters</u> of British people had access to it.

2) The availability of the Internet has meant that people now have access to more <u>information</u> than ever before.

3) It has changed the way people communicate. <u>Email</u> and <u>social networking</u> sites mean that users can <u>communicate</u> with others instantly, wherever they live.

4) <u>Online shopping</u> has become very popular. In 2011, <u>60%</u> of British adults made purchases online — more than France, Germany or the USA. This has created lots of opportunities for <u>businesses</u>, who can sell their goods <u>all over the world</u> through their websites.

5) The increase in Internet use has led to new problems, including fears over Internet <u>security</u>, online credit card <u>fraud</u> and the risk of <u>identity theft</u>.

Global Warming has led to a rise in Green Technology

1) There has been growing concern over <u>global warming</u> and the effect that <u>human activity</u> is having on the planet's climate.

2) There has been a lot of research into <u>renewable energy</u> such as wind and solar power. There has been an increase in the number of <u>wind farms</u> in the UK, such as the Barrow Offshore Wind Farm, which started operating in 2006.

3) <u>Hybrid cars</u>, (which include an electric motor to reduce the amount of petrol used) are also growing in popularity. Over <u>12,000 hybrid cars</u> were sold in the UK in 2012.

We live in an age of instant-access information...

Technology will continue to advance, and to change the way we live and work.

Sources and Questions

The welfare state and immigration can be pretty tricky topics to get your head around. These questions should help strengthen your knowledge.

1 *In 1911, Liberal Prime Minister David Lloyd George passed the National Insurance Act, which would provide security for the ill, the old and the unemployed.*

Source A — A poster about the National Insurance Act

Source B — A cartoon about David Lloyd George

Study both sources. Do the sources have the same attitude towards the Liberal reforms? Explain your answer using information from the sources.

2 *In 1948, the Labour government set up the National Health Service. Not everyone supported the NHS, but it became very popular.*

Source A — The man walking down the street is Aneurin Bevan, the minister in charge of founding the NHS.

What does this source suggest about opposition to the NHS?

Sources and Questions

3 *From 1945 it became clear that there was a shortage of workers in Britain. Immigrants from places like the West Indies, India and Pakistan were encouraged to settle in Britain.*

Source A — Newly arrived West Indian immigrants in Southampton

© Haywood Magee/Getty Images

Source B — A historian lists reasons why people migrated to the UK

1) Immigrants from the West Indies, India and Pakistan often lived in poverty in their homeland.
2) Britain needed people to work in hotels, hospitals, and the transport industry.
3) There were unskilled jobs in Britain which British workers did not want to do.
4) Britain needed more workers to help recovery after World War II.
5) Some British employers even paid for immigrants to come to do these jobs.

a) The family in Source A have arrived in England to start a new life.
Which of these words do you think best describe what they would be feeling? Pick two.

   excited   nervous   resentful   bored   confused   curious   frightened

b) Using Source B, name three places from which many immigrants came after 1945.

c) Using Source B, give two reasons why immigrants were encouraged to come to Britain after 1945.

4 *Many immigrants who came to Britain after World War Two experienced racism. Look at Source A and answer the question below.*

Source A — Racist graffiti in London

© Mary Evans Picture Library/ROGER MAYNE

What does Source A tell you about the treatment some immigrants received in Britain?

Summary Questions

From World War One to touch-screen mobile phones — this is another jam-packed section. It's important stuff though, stuff that's really shaped the world we live in now. So don't let all that juicy historical knowledge go over your head — have a go at these questions to help it sink in.

1) Which countries made up the Triple Entente?

2) The shooting of which Austrian Duke began the move towards World War One?

3) Write three sentences to describe what life would have been like in the trenches during World War One.

4) What was the name of the treaty that Germany had to sign in 1919?

5) What was the name of the organisation which was set up after the end of World War One to try and find peaceful solutions to international problems?

6) What was the name of the famous 1929 stock market crash in the USA?

7) Which area of England was least affected by the 1930s depression?

8) What was the name of the unemployment benefit in 1930s Britain?

9) Which organisation organised hunger marches to London throughout the 1930s?

10) What was "Anschluss"?

11) In what year did Hitler invade Poland?

12) When was rationing introduced in Britain?

13) Who became Prime Minister of Britain in 1940?

14) Name three ways the Jews were persecuted by the German government after Hitler came to power.

15) Use three sentences to describe what you think the ghetto in Warsaw might have been like.

16) Write a paragraph to explain what happened to Anne Frank's family from July 1942 onwards.

17) Approximately how many people were killed by the Nazis' "Final Solution"?

18) Who was put on trial at the Nuremburg Trials after World War Two?

19) What were the three main religious groups in India before independence?

20) Who led the peaceful demands for Indian independence?

21) What country was created when India was split in 1947?

22) Which country is the Suez Canal in?

23) Why was the Suez Canal so important to Britain?

24) In what year did the Easter Rising take place in Ireland?

25) In what year did the Liberal government introduce state pensions?

26) Imagine that you're a British ship builder in 1911. Write two sentences explaining how you think you'll benefit from the National Insurance Act.

27) In what year was the NHS introduced?

28) What was pre-fabricated housing?

29) In what year did the passengers of the Empire Windrush arrive in Britain?

30) What happened in Notting Hill in the summer of 1958?

31) Why was the three-day working week introduced in 1974?

32) Who was Britain's first female Prime Minister?

33) In what year was the World Wide Web launched?

34) In 2013, what percentage of adults in Britain owned a mobile phone?

Section One — Medieval Britain, 1066-1509

Pages 12-15

1) a) i) William promised to follow existing laws and customs.
     ii) He rewarded the Church with land.
     iii) He also rewarded the Normans with land.
   b) They built forts as a show of strength and to help assert control. It was important to do this because they were heavily outnumbered by the Saxons.

2) a) As a result of William's 'Harrying of the North' there was a very serious famine and about 100,000 people died of starvation.
   b) One advantage of William enforcing law and order harshly was that people could travel the land feeling safe, even if they were carrying a lot of money.

3) a) i) Five.
     ii) Seven.
     iii) Twenty-four.
   b) Firstly, it told him how much tax he would expect to get from each town or village. Secondly, it told him how many knights he could expect from each place if he called up the army.
   c) Source A is a primary source because it is from the Domesday Book itself (i.e. it is evidence that comes directly from that time in history). Source B is a secondary source because it is a modern viewpoint about that time in history.

4) a) The King granted land to 100 important clergy and 200 nobles — 300 people altogether.
   b) King
       ↓
      Nobles and clergy
       ↓
      Knights and gentry
       ↓
      Peasants
       ↓
      Slaves

5) a) The freestone was from Caen and Reigate.
   b) Churches were built from stone and other strong materials like iron and cement. It seems that care was taken to get the right stone from different places. Large sums of money were spent to build Westminster Abbey. It is therefore not surprising that many medieval churches survive today.

6) a) A relic is part of a dead saint's body or clothing, for example, a thorn from Christ's crown or St Agatha's thigh bone. Relics were believed to be powerful and to help with people's prayers.
   b) The relics probably weren't genuine.
      Possible reasons:
      1. It was a very long time since saints and Jesus had died, over such a long time these things would probably have been lost or destroyed in an accident.
      2. They would be easy to fake with bits of wood, or bones from the butcher or church yard.
      3. Jesus and saints were mostly from the Middle East — it seems unlikely things would travel so far.
   c) ii) Made up — maybe the author of this source wanted to show the Bishop in a bad light.

7) a) iii) They might have been angry that a member of the clergy should be so rich, when the clergy were supposed to live a religious life of poverty and restraint.
   b) They had to pay substantial taxes to the Church, and were pressured into paying through threats about the afterlife.

Pages 24-27

1) a) He made the barons obey him and pulled down some of their castles.
   b) The Archbishop refused to obey the King's rules.
   c) The author of Source B seems sympathetic to Thomas à Becket. He describes the knights as "in fury", a negative expression. His description of Becket makes him seem brave and confirms his loyalty to the King.

2) a) Source A suggests that the Third Crusade was a failure because King Richard became ill, his troops nearly starved to death and he failed to capture Jerusalem.
   b) No, Source B does not agree with Source A that the Third Crusade was a failure. It says that despite not capturing Jerusalem there were some successes.
   c) ii) a guess — the historian can only imagine what Richard was thinking.

3) a) In Source A Saladin is described as cruel, sometimes cheating, cold and without morals (unscrupulous).

    b) In Source B Saladin is described as strong, resourceful, courageous, humorous, loyal, admired by his followers, successful in war, courteous, generous and brave.

4) a) Any reasonable rewording e.g.
        1. Trials should be held quickly and people shouldn't be imprisoned without trial.
        2. Taxes would be made fairer.
        3. The King wouldn't interfere with the Church.
        4. Merchants wouldn't be made to pay unfair taxes.

    b) Source B shows King John was cruel by giving two examples of his cruelty: hanging and starving twenty-eight hostages and starving William de Braose's wife and child to death.

5) a) ii) The English controlled Wales by force — by building castles and making local lords powerful.

    b) Source B says the March Lords were important because they could react to problems in Wales quickly. This was important because there were a lot of rebellions in Wales.

6) a) The advantages of the clan system, according to Source B, were that clans protected their members and could quickly raise armies. The disadvantages, according to the sources, were that the clans could be bribed and constantly switched sides, making any rebellion weak.

    b) English kings could bribe Scottish lords to support them, which would weaken any rebellion. They could also put down rebellions with force, as Edward I did in Berwick.

    c) Two of:
        • To protect their clan from England, and avoid English attacks by siding with them.
        • Clans could become rich and powerful by taking bribes from England.
        • To get revenge on a rival clan.

    d) ii) Life for medieval Scots was hard. There was a lot of war and violence, but people were protected by their clan, who made sure that everyone had food and help when they needed it.

Pages 36-37

1) a) iii) Opinion.

    b) Source B uses observation — it says a ship from Gascony called at a harbour in Dorset and one of the sailors had the plague. Source A says the plague came from God — it doesn't give any reason for this opinion.

    c) 1. Swellings / boils appear at groin or armpits.
        2. Boils start to spread over the body.
        3. Black or red patches appear on the arms or thighs.

2) a) People were unhappy because of:
        1. the poll tax.
        2. the feudal system.
        3. the war with France.

    b) Possible answer:
        The Peasants' Revolt took place in 1381. Parliament tried to impose a heavy poll tax. People in Norfolk, Essex and Kent rebelled. They were led by Wat Tyler and John Ball. The rebels entered London but many went home again after promises made by the King. The rebels who stayed were defeated and their leaders were killed.

3) a) She believed that it was her duty to fight the English because she had been sent to do so by God.

    b) iii) They didn't believe her.

    c) ii) Source A suggests that Joan of Arc was determined to drive the English out of France at any cost, whereas Source B suggests that she seemed an unlikely hero at first.

4) Yes, the statement is supported by Sources A and B. Source A shows the two sides fighting each other, and one man is already dead on the ground. Source B says that "many" blows were dealt, "men were slain" and the Prince, Edward, was killed. All of these incidents are very violent.

Section Two — Tudors and Stuarts, Britain 1509-1745

Pages 47-49

1) a) The Church was central to the village community. It conducted important religious ceremonies, and organised education and help for the poor.
   b) According to Source B Henry VIII wanted to divorce Catherine of Aragon so he could marry Anne Boleyn, and the Pope wouldn't allow it.
   c) The statement is false — Source A shows that the Church was very important to people's lives.

2) a) Peace and stability.
   b) Treating Catholics harshly might frighten other Catholics so they'd be put off plotting against Elizabeth.

3) a) ii) That Mary had betrayed her.
   b) Source B suggests that Mary was brave at her execution. She comforts her two women even though she is the one who is going to die, and tells them not to cry for her.

4) a) iii) Elizabeth's policy in Ireland was often violent, and had a lot to do with religion.
   b) Source B suggests that the Irish are a brutal people who kill others in horrible ways, and that they have betrayed the Englishmen who cared for them. The author was serving Elizabeth in Ireland, so he might want to present the Irish like this to encourage English people to hate them, and support Elizabeth in crushing their rebellions.

5) a) A husband would help run the country and get Elizabeth pregnant to provide an heir.
   b) Philip of Spain means things that he believes only men can do, such as governing the country.
   c) iii) Opinion.

6) a) The author of Source A is Spanish. He is sorry that the Armada had to withdraw. He says that his fleet was harried from the enemy's country (i.e. England).
   b) Source B is by an Englishman. It describes "our ships" as having suffered "little hurt", while the Spanish ships have been damaged.

Pages 60-61

1) a) Source A.
   b) The source states that there were fewer treason trials, no revolts and fewer riots.
   c) False. Source A says short-term causes were responsible for the Civil War, but Source B says that the causes went back further in time.

2) a) *Two of the following* —
   • dissolves Parliament in 1655
   • forces MPs to sign an agreement recognising him as Protector;
   • excludes over 100 MPs from Parliament.
   b) He refused the Crown when it was offered to him by Parliament in 1657.

3) a) Parliamentarians.
   b) The **Parliamentarians** won the Civil War for a number of reasons.
   Reason 1
   They controlled **London** and the South East of England where there was a large population and more wealth than in other areas.
   Reason 2
   The Royalist army was very **divided** and had low morale.
   Reason 3
   Another country, **Scotland**, supported the Parliamentarian side.
   Reason 4
   The Royalist leader was **Charles I**. He was not a very good military leader. The Parliamentarians had better leaders like **Fairfax** and **Oliver Cromwell**.
   Reason 5
   The Parliamentarians were very well organised. Their army was called the **New Model Army**.

Pages 70-71

1) a) ii) Unsuccessful.
   b) Both sources agree that James II attacked the Church of England. Both say that he had personal failings as a ruler — Source A says he took opposition to his policies personally, and Source B says he was easily influenced. Both say he wanted to rule without any restraint on his power — Source A says he believed in the "divine right" of monarchs, and Source B says James was "in favour of rougher methods".

2) a) ii) Less numerous and not as well trained as William's.
   b) The writer wants readers to be impressed by William. He/she shows that:
   • William was brave.
   • He was not frightened by the bullet.
   • William's men looked up to him. They were relieved when they saw he wasn't dead.
   • William was tough. He stayed in the saddle for nineteen hours on the trot.

3) a) They were worried Scotland would be absorbed into England through the Union — because England was more powerful than Scotland.
   b) The Scottish MPs, because they were offered money to agree to the Union.

4) a) Motivated and ambitious
   b) At the time of the 1745 rebellion Charles Stuart was very ambitious and thought he had a chance of beating the English. In later life, according to Source B, he became an "alcoholic drifter".
   He was bad-tempered and became unpopular with his supporters.

Section Three — Industry, Empire and Reform, Britain 1745-1914

Pages 84-85

1) a) i) Yes.
      ii) Yes.
      iii) No.
      iv) Yes.
      v) No.
   b) The Empire included many hot countries in which produce like bananas and dates would grow. The shop in Source B has these goods because of trade with other countries in the Empire.

2) a) True. The colonists felt that they needed to draw up a list of rights and send them to the King. This suggests they felt that their rights had been taken from them by the British.
   b) The Sources suggest that the War of Independence broke out because of a disagreement about rights. The colonists felt that their rights as British citizens had been violated, but George III didn't agree, so he saw their actions as rebellious.

3) a) True.
   b) In Source B, Olaudah Equiano describes the "brutal cruelty" of the white slave traders, the heat, and the feeling of suffocation caused by overcrowding.

4) a) In order to collect evidence of atrocities committed by the slave traders.
   b) He was an MP and helped support the anti-slavery cause in Parliament. For example, he presented bills to Parliament for the abolition of the slave trade.

Pages 94-97

1) a) i) They were writing to the factory owner because they had heard that he had shearing frames.
      ii) The Luddites were threatening to destroy the machines if they were not removed. They also threatened to murder the machine owner if any of the Luddites were shot at. They made the same threats to the neighbours if their machines / shearing frames were not taken down.
      iii) It is from a group. *Evidence that it is a group could include* —
      • they mention 300 men;
      • they refer to lieutenants;
      • signed by a General of the Army of Redressers etc.
      iv) The author of the source would not want to give his identity away as he was talking about a criminal act and would not want to get caught.
   b) Machine breaking was a 'capital crime' — hanging was the punishment. A young boy was hanged for acting as a lookout, even though he wasn't directly involved in the machine-breaking.

2) a) i) Scotland — partly industrialised.
      ii) Wales — partly industrialised.
      iii) Southern England — partly industrialised.
      iv) Northern England — partly industrialised.
      v) The Midlands — heavily industrialised.
   b) i) Scotland — partly industrialised.
      ii) Wales — partly industrialised.
      iii) Southern England — partly industrialised.
      iv) Northern England — heavily industrialised.
      v) The Midlands — heavily industrialised.

c) Not all of Britain was evenly industrialised. Scotland and Wales were least industrialised. The South of England had more industry, but the most heavily industrialised areas, with the most canals and large towns were the Midlands and the North of England.

3) a) Source C describes houses like those depicted in Source A.
One reason for choice needed, for example:
- each house overcrowded
- houses packed close together

b) i) Evidence of overcrowding —
- houses packed close together
- number of people in back yards and windows

ii) Evidence of lack of hygiene —
- overcrowding — sheer number of people in small space
- hanging up washing in polluted air (from chimneys, trains etc).

iii) Evidence of pollution —
- smoke and noise from train
- smoke from chimneys

c) i) Evidence of overcrowding: 10 people to every house.

ii) Evidence of lack of hygiene:
- overcrowding
- no water supply
- no toilets

d) One example of middle class housing being preferable:
- more space between houses
- one family per house

4) a) Source A suggests that people visited Brighton for medical reasons on the advice of Dr Russell and his claim that drinking and bathing in sea water was good for you.

b) Five examples of leisure activities (there are others):
- library — learning, reading, lectures.
- park — strolling, flowers.
- pier — entertainments, walking out to enjoy 'sea air'.
- aquarium — looking at sea-life.
- railway — trips along sea front.

c) The downside of visiting Brighton was that it was too popular (especially with Londoners) and so was probably rather crowded and hectic.

d) Postcard should include details of activities from answer to b) and perhaps reference to the fact it is very popular and busy (using Source C). Perhaps reference made to pleasure of leaving London for fresh sea air and healthy leisure options. Lots to see and do, e.g. beautiful pavilion, park, seaside.

Pages 106-107

1) a) i) Disraeli felt that a larger number of people deserved the vote because they had skills and ideas which they should be allowed to voice.

b) The speech in Source C.

c) No. In Source B, voting reform is portrayed as 'A Leap in the Dark', and this is a cartoon, which suggests that a lot of people were worried about reform, not just politicians.

d) iii) They didn't know what would happen as a result.

2) a) i) Well-educated, responsible, worthwhile.
ii) Immoral, criminal, irresponsible.

b) i) Women can't vote. Even if a woman is a mayor or a doctor she can't vote.
Men can vote. Even if they have been drunkards or criminals men can vote.

3) a) Source A suggests that suffragettes threw stones at shop windows — so they were prepared to break the law and damage other people's property to get their cause noticed.

b) Lucy Burns was treated badly in prison.
The answer should include at least one example to back up this claim, e.g.
- She was forced to undress.
- She was knocked down.
- Her hair was pulled.
- The women were dragged to their cells.

ANSWERS

Section Four — Britain and the Wider World, 1900 to the Present Day

Pages 114-115

1) a) Germany, Italy and Austria.
   b) Italy is seen as less important. It is trying to reach the level of the others.
   c) The murder of the heir to the Austrian throne.

2) a) Gas fumes were green and thick, like a sea, in which men couldn't breathe, so they 'drowned'.
   b) Two of the following —
   • The gas struck quickly.
   • It could kill by choking.
   • It could make you blind.

3) a) Any three of the following —
   • It had to pay money to other countries.
   • It had no air force.
   • It had a very small navy.
   • Its army was much smaller.
   • It lost lands it had gained.
   b) Source B shows some German people couldn't even afford to buy essentials like food — Germany was already poverty-stricken because of the war. The huge damages payment would make Germany even poorer.

4) a) The sources suggest that people thought the League was a weak force. Source A suggests that it faced too big a challenge. Source B says it couldn't cope with big conflicts.
   b) Japan, Italy and Germany.
   c) No. It did have success settling arguments in countries like Greece.

Page 119

1) a) iii) The Wall Street Crash caused widespread alarm.
   b) Source A says that it was 'the worst day in stock market history', and known as 'Black Thursday'. This suggests it was a very bad day for people. In Source B, the headline uses the word 'panic', which supports the fact that there was alarm.

2) a) Unemployed workers in the 1930s received very little money from unemployment benefits. This meant they often struggled to feed their families.
   b) The sources show that not everyone was affected equally by the depression. In Source A there are unemployed men marching against starvation, while in Source B there are people who are well dressed who can afford to go out to dinner and a show.
   c) Unemployed workers did not like the means test. The speaker quoted in the source calls it 'dirty' and says that it needs 'smashing'. The means test often led to people's dole payments being cut and, as the source says, 'starvation' and 'degradation'.

Pages 126-127

1) a) German, Hitler, money, industry.
   b) These sources disagree with each other. Source D denies that Hitler used threats to take power in Austria and suggests it was what people wanted — but Source C claims that Hitler threatened to invade Austria.
   c) These sources both suggest that the expansion of Germany wasn't popular. Source C claims Hitler had to threaten the Austrians to allow him to take power, and Source B shows a Sudeten woman crying as the Nazis arrived (although it is possible she is crying with joy).

2) a) The government thought that bombing would cause a lot of damage in London and they didn't want children to be hurt or killed.
   b) ii) Churchill was determined to win the war and encouraged people in Britain to keep a fighting spirit.

Pages 134-135

1) a) Jews were mistreated by being housed in overcrowded conditions and being refused permission to practise their religion.
   b) Source A says the Jews were mistreated because the Germans wanted to break their spirit and make them lose hope.
   c) The Polish Police official in Source B believes that members of the police were prepared to harm Jews out of hatred. He claims that they wanted revenge, though he does not say why.
   He also believes that the police were greedy to get their hands on Jewish wealth, and that is another reason for the police action.

2) a) 1. Planned starvation.
   2. Epidemics, such as typhus.
   b) Possible answer — Conditions were terrible. The camp was overcrowded and there was little food, clothing or medicine. Many people were ill with diseases like typhus.

3) a) The Nazis persecuted the Roma because they believed they were "an inferior race" and therefore couldn't be "good Germans".
   b) 1935 — The Roma were classified as 'aliens' by the Nazis.
   1939 — Roma were sent to concentration camps in Poland.
   1942 — They were taken to a Roma concentration camp which was part of the Auschwitz-Birkenau camp.
   1944 — The SS shot all the Roma in Auschwitz before they could be freed by the Russian army.

4) a) ii) Source A shows that at least one of the people responsible for the death camps was put on trial. Photographs are limited as evidence — they leave out a lot of information.
   b) Source B gives the further information that Eichmann was only put on trial after Israeli agents kidnapped him in 1960. He was tried in Jerusalem, found guilty and executed in 1962.

Pages 140-141

1) a) Source A shows that Gandhi is resisting the British, but the blunt tusks show that he is doing it peacefully.
   b) The saying suggests that if you respond to violence with violence, everyone will lose.
   c) Gandhi was trying to show that you could legally and peacefully rebel against Britain. If Britain was charging tax on buying salt, you could find your own salt.

2) a) Hindus, Sikhs and Muslims.
   b) Pakistan would be mostly inhabited by Muslims.
   c) Pakistan is unusual because it is split into two countries — West and East Pakistan, divided by India.

3) The illustrator thinks that the Suez crisis would end in violence and death. You can tell this because the water has been labelled 'blood red', the figures representing France and Britain are armed and the face of the sphinx has the face of a skull.

4) a) i) An example of carefully planned violence is the killing of the British agents by the IRA.
   ii) The Black and Tans firing into a crowd was revenge killing.
   b) iii) Source A seemed unbiased, as it is condemning the actions of both the IRA and the British.

Pages 150-151

1) The sources disagree on the Liberal reforms. Source A suggests that the Liberal reforms will bring positive changes. The poster is titled 'the dawn of hope' which is very optimistic. It shows Lloyd George explaining the benefits to a man who is unwell and who would receive help under the reforms. Source B is not so positive about the reforms. It shows Lloyd George as a highway man. This suggests that the cartoonist think Lloyd George is stealing from taxpayers in order to fund his reforms.

2) Source A shows us that many doctors opposed the creation of the NHS. In the source we can see the doctors on Harley Street waiting to trip up Aneurin Bevan, the minister in charge of founding the NHS.

3) a) Any two of...excited, nervous, confused, curious, frightened.
   b) West Indies, India and Pakistan.
   c) Immigrants were encouraged because...
   • Workers were needed after WW2.
   • There were lots of unskilled jobs which British people wouldn't do.

4) Source A shows racist graffiti in London. The photograph suggests that immigrants were not welcomed by some people and were sometimes the target of racist abuse.

Index

Index

Index

Acknowledgements

The publisher would like to thank the following —

Page 12 Q1, Source A — A Briggs 'A Social History of Britain'. Weidenfeld & Nicolson, a division of the Orion Publishing Group. 1999.

Page 13 Q3, Source B — 'Living Through History, Foundation Book 1, Medieval Realms', Nigel Kelly, Rosemary Rees and Jane Shuter, Pearson Education Limited.

Page 14 Q6, Source A — Tony McAleavy 'Medieval Britain' (1991) Cambridge University Press

Page 15 Q7, Source B — www.historylearningsite.co.uk

Page 22 Image and Written Source — © British Library Board

Page 24 Q1 Source A — R.J. Unstead (1968) 'Looking at History', Q2 Source A — Marshall Cavendish Ltd (1995) 'Exploring the past: the Middle Ages', Q2 Source B — Extract from 'The Crusades' by Ian Dawson (OUP, 1992), copyright © Ian Dawson 1992, reprinted by permission of Oxford University Press.

Page 25 Q3, Source A — 'The Crusades', Z Oldenbourg. The Orion Publishing Group, London, Q3, Source B — 'The Crusades' Reprinted by permission of HarperCollins Publishers Ltd © 1992, Fiona Macdonald, Q4 Source A — © British Library Board Q4 Source B — Text adapted from: http://www.bbc.co.uk/history/british/middle_ages/john_01.shtml 'King John' written by Dr. Mike Ibeji

Page 26 Q5, Source A — Chepstow Castle Image reproduced with kind permission of Robert Harding

Page 37 Q3, Source B — Excerpt from "The First Chronicle to Record Joan of Arc's Exploits" in The First Biography of Joan of Arc, translated and annotated by Daniel Rankin and Claire Quintal © 1964. Reprinted by permission of the University of Pittsburgh Press

Page 47 Q1, Source A — 'The Making of the UK' , Joe Scott, Pearson Education Limited, Q1, Source B — R. J. Unstead (1968) 'Looking at History', Q2, Source A — Thomas, Heather, The Life and Times of Queen Elizabeth I, elizabethi.org, 1998-2014

Page 48 Q4 Source B — The National Archives Website used under the terms of the open government licence http://www.nationalarchives.gov.uk/doc/open-government-licence/version/3/

Page 49 Q5 Source A — Thomas, Heather, The Life and Times of Queen Elizabeth I, elizabethi.org, 1998-2014

Page 60 Q1, Source A — John Morrill 'What was the English Revolution?' History Today, Volume: 34, Issue: 3 March 1984, Q1, Source B — 'CAUSES OF THE ENGLISH CIVIL WAR by Conrad Russell (1990) By permission of Oxford University Press'

Page 61 Q3, Source B — Angus Stroud, A Modern Historian, 'Stuart England', 1999, pages 103-104 Published by Routledge 1999.

Page 70 Q2 Source A and Source B — The Director of Services, The Grand Orange Lodge of Ireland, Belfast, Northern Ireland

Page 80 Evidence on Slave Trade 1790, Source: The National Archives Website used under the terms of the open government licence http://www.nationalarchives.gov.uk/doc/open-government-licence/version/3/

Page 83 'Garden Lane Fruit Shop in the early 1900s'. Image used with permission from Cheshire Archives and Local Studies and Chester History and Heritage, http://www.cheshireimagebank.org.uk

Page 84 Q1 Source B — 'Garden Lane Fruit Shop in the early 1900s'. Image used with permission from Cheshire Archives and Local Studies and Chester History and Heritage, http://www.cheshireimagebank.org.uk

Page 85 Q4 Source A — 'Britain and the Slave Trade', Rosemary Rees, Pearson Education Limited

Page 94 Q1 Source B, 'Expansion, Trade and Industry 1750-1900' (Hodder & Stoughton, 1993) © 1993 J.F. Aylett.

Page 97 Q4, Source A — 'The Work of Dr Richard Russell' © Ted Power, Q4, Source B — 'Peace and War' (Hodder Murray, 1993). C. Colin Shephard, Andy Reid, Keith Shephard.

Page 107 Q1 Source A — "What a woman may be and yet not have a vote, What a man may have been and yet not lose the vote". Britain, 1920 - © Victoria and Albert Museum, London, Q3 Source A — 'Suffragettes and Votes for Women', L.E. Snellgrove, Pearson Education Limited, Q2 Source B — 'LUCY BURNS: A suffragette in Holloway Prison', from 'Eyewitness: The 20th century', 1994, edited by Jon E. Lewis, Constable & Robinson by kind permission of Constable & Robinson

Page 119 Q2 Source C — Hunger March Speech reused under the terms of The Open Government Licence: http://www.nationalarchives.gov.uk/doc/open-government-licence/version/3/

Acknowledgements

Page 121 Quote by Chamberlain reproduced under the terms of the Open Government Licence http://www.nationalarchives.gov.uk/doc/open-government-licence/version/3/

Page 127 Q2 Source A — Poster "Children should be Evacuated" used under the terms of the Open Government Licence http://www.nationalarchives.gov.uk/doc/open-government-licence/version/3/, Q2 Source C — Winston Churchill Speech used Under the Terms of the Open Government Licecnce http://www.nationalarchives.gov.uk/doc/open-government-licence/version/3/

Page 130 Hell, Josef. "Aufzeichnung", 1922, ZS 640, p. 5, Institut für Zeitgeschichte, cited in Fleming, Gerald. Hitler and the Final Solution. Berkeley: University of California Press. 1984. p. 17, cited in "Joseph Hell on Adolf Hitler", The Einsatzgruppen.

Page 134 Q1 Source B — © Masters of Death by Richard Rhodes, Vintage Books, Copyright © 1995-2008 Random House, Inc. All rights reserved.

Page 135 Q3 Source A — The World After 1900 Reprinted by permission of Raintree

Page 141 Q3 Source A — Paine, Albert Bigelow Th. Nast: His Period and His Pictures (New York, NY: The Macmillan Company, 1904) Courtesy the private collection of Roy Winkelman, Q4 Source A — 'Modern Minds', James Byron, Christine Counsel, Michael Gorman, Derek People, Michael Riley, Pearson Education Limited © 1999

Page 150 National Insurance Act reused under the terms of The Open Government Licence: http://www.nationalarchives.gov.uk/doc/open-government-licence/version/3/

With thanks to Getty Images for permission to use the photos on pages 4, 5, 7, 11, 18, 20, 21, 33, 41, 43, 44, 46, 50, 55, 64, 67, 68, 85, 90, 96, 102, 103, 104, 111, 114, 115, 116, 119, 120, 121, 123, 124, 125, 126, 127, 128, 131, 133, 135, 142, 145, 146, 147, 148, 150, 151.

With thanks to Mary Evans Picture Library for permission to use the images on pages 6, 8, 10, 28, 31, 51, 53, 57, 58, 62, 65, 66, 76, 77, 79, 81, 87, 89, 90, 91, 92, 98, 100, 106, 111, 129, 137, 140, 151.

With thanks to iStockphoto for permission to use the image on page 149.

Every effort has been made to locate copyright holders and obtain permission to reproduce sources. For those sources where it has been difficult to trace the originator of the work, we would be grateful for information. If any copyright holder would like us to make an amendment to the acknowledgements, please notify us and we will gladly update the book at the next reprint. Thank you.